PLANNING A
SCIENTIFIC CAREER
IN INDUSTRY

PLANNING A SCIENTIFIC CAREER IN INDUSTRY

Strategies for Graduates and Academics

SANAT MOHANTY AND RANJANA GHOSH

A JOHN WILEY & SONS, INC., PUBLICATION

Library of Congress Cataloging-in-Publication Data:

Mohanty, Sanat S.
    Planning a scientific career in industry : strategies for graduates and
academics / Sanat Mohanty and Ranjana Ghosh.
        p. cm.
    Includes index.
    ISBN 978-0-470-46004-7 (pbk.)
    1. Science–Vocational guidance. 2. Science–Economic aspects. 3. Science
and industry. I. Ghosh, Ranjana. II. Title.
    Q147.M56   2010
    502.3–dc22   2009045864

10 9 8 7 6 5 4 3 2 1

CONTENTS

PREFACE

This book was written to address the questions and concerns of new graduates (and those getting there) about industrial careers. In the five years preceding this book, one of us had the opportunity to interact extensively with new graduates during the process of campus recruiting and hiring as well as through new employee orientation programs within the corporate world. We learned a few key things that got us thinking about these concerns:

- Graduating students usually understood in depth the technical problems with which companies of interest were engaged.
- However, among technical graduates (those graduating with degrees in science or technology) there was little understanding of the nuances of profit motives and strategies in the industry.
- There was also little understanding of the importance of the organizational structure and the culture of the company.
- Hence, there was little or no appreciation of the nature of solutions to problems or the importance of different kinds of problems having varied relevance to industries based on the above-described nuances.

In not recognizing the complex and nonlinear connectedness of these aspects of corporate functioning, students were often not aware of how their choices in careers may or may not be aligned with their personal goals or how their choices in problem-solving strategies may or may not impact their careers in the way they desire.

We found a number of books on careers in the industry; often, however, they were prescriptive in nature and attempted to address specific details of how you might want to present yourself to your team or your boss, or how you might want to establish your credentials without the context of the larger picture of the industry and of the specific organization.

Thus, we set out to write this book to address key questions we felt were left unanswered. At the very outset, we decided not to write a prescriptive book because such a book can be limiting. Such linear descriptions of career strategies could never capture the complex and nonlinear framework of functions and relationships in the industry within which careers evolve. We felt that our audience of graduating students looking for industrial jobs are analytical and aware and that our role should be to describe the various components of the industry, the functions of these components, the relationship between them, and the forces that define its environment. We understood that the definition of success would also be highly varied; for some, it may imply becoming a vice president of a large company, for another it might imply a stable job that allowed other activities. Our audience of technical graduates have the wherewithal—we believe—to base complex decisions for their specific situations based on an understanding of this framework.

The book was based on key input from a large number of people in over 20 companies spanning a variety of industries. These inputs on a variety of issues—from the nature of strategies, organizational structure, and cultures to the nature of new employment programs—helped us understand the breadth of this framework. These inputs also helped share tools and strategies that are used by groups and individuals in these companies to address some of the very same questions that you have as you start your career. The book is peppered with numerous anecdotes of real-life situations highlighting these strategies.

This book thus describes the goals of different companies in an industry, their varied profit goals, and the strategies they choose to achieve them. In implementing these strategies, they choose organizational structures (which then also evolve over time) and build a culture—the DNA of an organization. These closely define the nature and viability of career choices—that is, the value of specific skills, whether you are looking for a high-growth fast-paced career or a more relaxed career. They often influence the success of choices you make in solving specific problems or advancing a project. In addition to providing the framework described above, this book also presents you with a variety of tools and strategies that may help you find your answers in helping you start in a company, establishing yourself, and navigating the industrial career.

Over the last decade, various industries have seen numerous economic ups and downs. For new employees, this often implies intermittent hiring freeze and a slowdown in career growth. However, we believe that understanding of the framework within which industries operate can help a new employee better deal with such changes and position himself or herself for a more effective career management.

We would like to acknowledge discussions with numerous friends, colleagues, and professionals across the industry who shared their experiences and analysis, providing richness to this book.

SANAT MOHANTY
RANJANA GHOSH

THINKING ABOUT CAREERS

The last few decades have seen an increasing complexity in career options—it is no longer just choices between being a lawyer, a doctor, or an engineer. Even within industrial organizations, there are more positions connecting to numerous functional needs with defined roles and expertise. Organizations do not just look for chemists, but also look for surface analytical chemists, synthetic polymer chemists, or small-molecule synthetic chemists (among a dozen other descriptions if not more). Industries today look not only for project managers, but also for project managers who have had experience in regulated industries and have worked on implantable devices. This perhaps reflects the increasing complexity of problems and levels of specialization necessary to solve them.

To a new graduate or to someone who has recently started his or her industrial career, this presents a threat and an opportunity. It is not just the increased technical complexity of industrial problems—which someone graduating with an advanced degree or with some research experience will appreciate—but also the significant complexity in business issues and organizational structure.

Planning a Scientific Career in Industry: Strategies for Graduates and Academics
By Sanat Mohanty and Ranjana Ghosh
Copyright © 2010 John Wiley & Sons, Inc.

A few years ago, an industrial group (of which I was a part) was engaged in theoretically predicting the behavior of surface-modified nanoparticles in solvent dispersions. We knew that the chemical nature of the modifying agents made a big difference. When we changed from alcohol functionalities to acid functionalities, or sometimes even when we changed the isomers in the surface modifying groups, the stability of the dispersions changed. We were struggling to understand how we could theoretically predict the behavior of these dispersions and presented this problem to a leading academic expert in this area. He said that while they had done much with model systems, they had not looked at the impact of such complex chemistries—after all they had the choice of ignoring these problems. We did not have that choice, because our real products needed understanding of real chemistries. We eventually did resolve the problem and that helped us predict the behavior of such particles, but we did not dot all the i's and cross the t's until much later. The necessity of solving more difficult problems drove us to explore a richness in science that would have otherwise passed us by. But even in doing so, there were a number of associated phenomena and questions that we did not answer—we did not have the time. And we have not gone back to answer those questions.

Problems in school are more of an exploratory nature— even when they have a specific goal. No product plan or sales expectations are tied to their resolution. Problems in the industrial sector, however, have a significant amount riding on their resolution—deadlines and pressures associated with deadlines become significant. Success or failure can cost an organization credibility in the marketplace and affect business plans. In the race to meet these deadlines, one often does not have the time or opportunity to understand every associated phenomenon; thus progress is often driven by good approximations—tested heuristically or by performance metrics.

At the same time, though it may sound contradictory, details are much more important in the industry than in academia. For example, what are the impurities in the raw material stream? How does the reaction system change with changing different components? How much energy is required? What is the kinetics of a process and what is the economic viability? These details may not matter in a laboratory setting but may mark the difference between a successful program and a failed one.

Industrial jobs are highly open-ended. There is no closure at the end of a semester or a year or even a thesis. One does not always know where the end of your project may be or what would even define the end. Sometimes even the customer does not know what she wants—her initial ideas might change based on your results. One does not know what one may find and how that may change the trajectory or even the nature of the program. Such open-endedness of programs and plans also affects performance appraisal processes (as a new graduate will learn, this is one key component of career growth). Your performance is rated before all the i's have been dotted—in fact, you may not even have the opportunity to dot all the i's. The key, then, is to manage one's performance through the ups and downs of a program in a way that highlights contributions throughout the process, not just at the end.

Besides, early achievement or failure is not an end state either. One's early successes may lead to greater focus on the program with more upper management visibility than it is ready for—it could lead to much greater expectations and, potentially, to a failure. Past failures or successes may impact expectations or impressions of one's effort. To repeat an earlier statement: Understanding and implementing performance management becomes important.

An individual is but one function of a very complex network focused on achieving an objective. This implies that rewards or even the nature of success is not straightforward. There are no promises of "do this and you will get that": One often does not know what one gets for doing something or where it might take one's career. Success is often less well defined. One's findings might result in proving that a certain technology is unfeasible, leading to the ending of a program. One's due diligence could lead to the team realizing that some other invention has been patented, and you should not be working on this approach. Are these successes?

One may have an invention; however, that may not lead to commercial success. There may be no use for this invention at that particular time, proper marketing plans may not be in place, or there might be miscommunication between various teams working on developing this technology further or the business climate that may lead to its stagnation or shelving.

In this seemingly chaotic environment, how does one become ready for an industrial career? What should one be thinking about or planning for? Can one even plan an industrial career—especially in today's world of *ad hoc* job elimination, month-by-month planning driven by Wall Street analysis? Is it even practical to ask and hope to rationally understand whether one is making the right choices in one's livelihood options such that these choices align with ones own needs or goals? If it is accepted that such careers and programs in the industry are nonlinear, is it feasible to aspire to do A or be B or make plans for what one needs to do to get there? Can one even hope to know if one really would fit into being B or whether doing A is a right choice?

One begins by recognizing that these are in fact opportunities, if one is ready for them—opportunities to try new roles and new functions, opportunities to challenge new problems, and opportunities to define and redefine oneself, to learn, adapt and grow, if one is ready. Challenges are opportunities to be continually successful. The nonlinearity allows for one to drive one's own career—simply because no one else can drive or define your career. Not because no one will want to but because the plethora of opportunities and the unpredictability of career trajectories makes it impossible for another person to do so. No one can say with any confidence "You are good at X; do the following and you will be successful." Industrial workplaces are strewn with brilliant but frustrated people who were not ready or did not adapt to the workplace that requires much more than just academic genius.

The complexity of functions and nonlinearity of opportunities requires that an individual recognize the environment, understand oneself, and be prepared by having multiple scenarios planned. It provides an opportunity to explore, experiment, and plan because one's career is not defined only by the first decision one takes. Let us look at a scenario of a generation or two ago where if you had joined as an engineer in an electrical company, your career path in this company was largely defined. You would, perhaps, have started on a project, and as you proved yourself, you would have been appointed into bigger projects and then at an appropriate time got your first promotion and there you would go. Once you started in one position, options of career trajectories were few. Your performance would define how far you would go within those few options.

In today's world, there are many more choices available with regard to the nature of your job. For example, with a degree in physics, you could as likely be a banker or a financial analyst as you might be a professor, a researcher, or a technical manager. Even your first job is not well-defined. Often, your job can change between when you are interviewed and when you start working. Jobs can change at any point based on volatility in the marketplace, change in a customer's needs, or business strategy. Even if your project is successful, it is impossible to predict what project you may be working on next year. There is more volatility in your career. Increasingly, you will find programs being shut down. Frequently, you will have to find new projects or new jobs. But these are also opportunities to reinvent yourself.

So, in such a situation, it is up to you to proactively define your career. The uncertainty can affect your career if you are not ready for it. However, if you are, it opens up avenues for change in ways that were not possible decades ago. To be ready, you need to understand the workplace and recognize opportunities to solve problems. More importantly, you need to spend enough time introspecting, understanding who you are, knowing your own needs and goals, knowing your passions, recognizing new skills that will help you grow, and learning to what extent you can adapt and what you can challenge. Stepping back for a moment, you can see why you need to truly understand the important factors in the working of a company in a specific industry and rigorously plan for what you truly want.

Consider your thesis: You began work on a difficult and somewhat new problem. You analyzed the work done in that area, you reviewed theories that worked and those that did not, and you identified the different aspects that worked or identified those that failed and those that may have had internal contradictions. Based on your analysis, you extended some theories with a hypothesis or two, or you developed new hypotheses and then tested them with experimental data or observations leading to some conclusions. You did not just go with a gut feeling on what you thought a new hypothesis might be. And yet, we often make our career decisions based on gut feeling. Often, such decisions are made on the basis of a single industrial experience, or experience of our academic advisers who may have limited understanding of or exposure to industrial processes, or even based on some recent experience that may have biased our instincts. If we take so much care to perform due diligence on a research project, should we not go through a similar process of analyzing the workplace and our own needs in planning our careers?

Planning for your career should be no different than an entrepreneur planning a start-up venture. You need to consider your life needs, your skills, your strengths and weaknesses, your market needs, and your access to networks and to the market, and you need to build strategic plans based on multiple scenarios that account for these factors.

You will invest a significant part of your conscious life, your intelligence, and your creativity in your career. Your sense of achievement and satisfaction will depend on your strengths, weaknesses, and needs and how those align with your career choices. Billions of people do not have the choice of choosing or shaping their careers. As a knowledge worker,[1] you do. You are privileged to be able to choose a career that is fulfilling. You can choose to value and take advantage of that privilege, or you could follow the crowd and miss out on opportunities that are right for you.

LAYOUT OF THE BOOK

The second chapter of this book introduces (a) the framework within which a technology company may be understood, (b) the industry within which it operates, and (c) jobs within this industry. While most readers with technical backgrounds would not be strangers to the technology industry, this chapter attempts to introduce business aspects of the industry and *how*

---

[1]Knowledge workers are employees engaged in primarily understanding or analyzing knowledge and shaping entities based on knowledge. Knowledge workers in today's workforce are valued for their ability to interpret information within a specific subject area. They will often advance the overall understanding of that subject through focused analysis, design, and/or development. They use research skills to define problems and to identify alternatives. Fueled by their expertise and insight, they work to solve those problems, in an effort to influence company decisions, priorities, and strategies.

business strategy frames jobs in the industry. It introduces the reader to choices that companies make in measuring their performance, their strategies, and positions in the marketplace as well as how they choose to organize themselves to succeed. While each of these areas requires multiple books for in-depth analysis, this chapter presents an overview while drawing the reader to the connections between these choices that a company makes and the nature of jobs as defined by these choices, provoking the reader to analyze the implication of such jobs vis-à-vis his or her own career goals and life needs.

The third chapter provides the framework to think about the nature and kind of jobs based on your own skills, personality, strengths, and life needs. It uses your life needs to provoke your passions and interests and then helps development of job maps based on your skills and strengths that overlap with these passions and align with your life needs. While it does not provide extensive tools for self-analysis[2,3] (there are numerous other books that effectively provide such analysis), it helps you understand skills needed in the market, the kinds of problems that the industry faces, and how your skills may be appropriately developed to solve those problems. It critiques the commonly held belief that specific jobs require specific personalities and suggests strategies that different personalities may use to solve problems effectively. Through these tools, it lays the groundwork to develop a strategy map to guide you through your needs and your ambitions.

The fourth chapter focuses on knowledge and tools relevant to you as you start out in the industry. Beginning

---

[2]B. Harrington and D. T. Hall, *Career Management and Work-Life Integration: Using Self Assessment to Navigate Contemporary Careers*, Sage Publications, 2007.

[3]I. B. Myer, *Gifts Differing: Understanding Personality Type*, Davies-Black Publishing, 1995.

with new employee orientation programs in companies, it describes the kind of knowledge that you should be looking for within these programs. Problem solving is your key strength, the biggest reason why you were hired; this chapter elaborates on more contextual and broader understanding of problem solving and how it defines your job. The chapter describes the role of performance metrics and processes of performance appraisal in the context of career growth. Your supervisor and your team are often key stakeholders in the appraisal process; the chapter talks about getting to know them, understanding your relationships with them, and managing expectations.

The fifth chapter focuses on processes and tools that help you establish yourself in your company. It begins by highlighting that as a new employee in a technology company, building your technical credibility is your first major goal and provides tools and strategies to manage technical projects and establish your technical credibility. Technical credibility is not just about your technical work; in recognizing this fact, the chapter includes discussions to help you understand communication and collaboration in an industrial environment and how you can leverage these processes better. Finally, it introduces you to your biggest support system in the industry: your network and your mentor(s).

The final chapter introduces a new employee to a broader and more complete vision of leadership and how that will help the new employee long term but must be learned and practiced right away. It introduces the new employee to the fact that she is a de facto leader in certain areas and responsibilities already. It shares modes of leadership that are not often idolized in popular media—such as consensus based and nonhierarchical forms of leadership. It also discusses how industry (and real life) always has multiple leadership needs that have multiple leadership skills and that good leaders often build multiple intelligences through practice.

This book is about you, how you could potentially plan a career that makes most sense to you, and empower you to build a career that aligns with your interests. It asks you what you want to do and asks whether that is really what you want to do or whether the opportunity cost of such activity is onerous. It also provides for strategies to plan and succeed at what those goals may be. Most importantly:

1. It attempts to define industrial careers through various parameters that are based on how the industry operates.

2. It provokes you to think about your own needs, skills, and expectations.

3. It provides you with tools and points you to resources to help you make choices and develop skills for a career that would be most fulfilling to you.

MEET THE INDUSTRY

Success in school is built on the ability to do well in tests—at least partially. It is also based on strong understanding in areas within a field that are relevant to some specific industry (at least for readers of this book). Hopefully, success in school is also based on creativity, discipline, and a growing ability to solve problems. Those traits are relevant in the industry. Problems in school are primarily technical or subject-related and usually well-defined. In graduate programs, students are exposed to open-ended problems and strategies to solve them including research, planning experiments, analysis, articulation of potential solutions or paths forward, and so on. Graduate programs and research experience also potentially expose students to multiple solutions with broad—and sometimes conflicting—implications.

The industry is a very different place from school. Success in industry needs skills learned at school and much more. It needs an understanding of the industrial workplace. Thus, any discussion on career planning in the industry must begin with an introduction to the industry.

No two industrial organizations are the same; in fact, often different sections of the same organization are different.

Planning a Scientific Career in Industry: Strategies for Graduates and Academics
By Sanat Mohanty and Ranjana Ghosh
Copyright © 2010 John Wiley & Sons, Inc.

11

However, there are certain features that are present (in varying degrees) in almost all technology-driven organizations. Understanding the framework within which we can define industrial activities can help us understand each industry and how we relate to jobs in these industries.

This book is intended for careers in technology—basic research, process and product development, technology management, and manufacturing and marketing activities that technologies support, as well as other activities that may support technology development. Companies, corporations, or other for-profit enterprises are of interest to us when technology development has a significant role. Activities related to development or acquisition of technologies are key to these organizations and are integral parts of their business model.[4]

This section introduces you—the new graduate or the student who will soon graduate—to the industry, pointing to some key parameters that are components of any industrial organization, and defines the ones of interest to you. This chapter describes various aspects of an organization. We recognize that you probably will not be making business decisions as you start out your career; however, all these aspects of a company's choices will affect your day-to-day work and your ability to meet your career goals. Some of these are aspects you can influence, whereas others you must understand and plan accordingly.

---

[4]Technology companies do not include media or finance or strategy consulting firms. Technology companies also do not include autonomous research labs (since these do not commercialize technology). Technology companies do include organizations that make and sell a wide variety of goods: electronic devices, medical devices, pharmaceuticals, soaps, chemicals, consumer goods, automobiles, and so on. Organizations that provide technology-based solutions to other organizations (but do not necessarily manufacture any product themselves) are also considered technology companies.

UNDERSTANDING AN ORGANIZATION

There are three important features of any company that one must recognize and analyze:

1. Companies are set up to make *profits*. Your job is to address challenges and create opportunities to help make profits.
2. *Strategies* are needed to make profits. The strategies used by a company defines the nature of jobs and the nature of challenges that jobs present. How do you contribute to the strategies of your organization?
3. *Organizational structure* in a company is based on its strategies and is a complex system. What is your role in the organization?

NATURE OF PROFITS

Any industrial organization is focused on making money. The first pointer to the company is its financial performance: How well does it meet the primary goals it has set out for itself. A large amount of financial data is available in the business domain— including the company's own submission to the Stock Exchange Commission (or similar body) if it is a publicly traded company, along with analyst reports. These will include analysis of various leverage and liquidity ratios,[5] return on

---

[5]Leverage ratio (which measures the extent to which the company's assets are financed with debt), liquidity ratio (which measures the company's ability to pay its bills), profitability ratio (which measures the company's ability to generate earnings), efficiency ratio (which measures the company's ability to utilize its assets), and market value ratio (which measures the market perception about the company's future prospects). These ratios are often used to further calculate the companies return on assets and return on equity.

ROA=(Net income/revenue)*(Revenue/assets)=Profit margin*Asset turnover

ROE = (Net income/revenue) * (Revenue/assets) * (Assets/equity) = ROA * Equity multiplier

assets and equity,[6] discounted cash flow, options modeling, and so on. These will probably be more informational than an analysis by a beginner; however, it may be useful to focus on some key aspects:

- What is the performance of the industry (is it a growing, stagnating, or dying industry)?
- What has been its long-term performance?
- How does the growth of the company compare with the growth of the market where this company participates?

It is necessary to understand these numbers in context. How have these ratios changed over time? Is the company becoming more efficient or less? For example, one could find key financial components of BP through a simple web search. The return on assets, for example, is 8.4% for BP and the return on equity is 25.78% for the first quarter of 2008.[7] Are these numbers good or bad? Have they become better? How much variation exists in these numbers from year to year? How do the numbers change during times of economic growth and times of downturn? Does the company do better or worse than the average market during difficulty times? Does the company take advantage of good times? To make sense of these numbers, it is also necessary to compare with its competitors (Exxon, Shell, etc.) and with the market in general. Besides providing input on the financial health of the company, this analysis also gives us an understanding about the leadership of the company.

Different organizations may value their successes differently: Some value[8] the total money they make, or the total profit,

---

[6]Simple online models and tools are available to estimate the financial health of a company.

[7]http://finance.yahoo.com/q/ks?s=BP.

[8]A note by McKinsey and Company, Inc. on how companies strategically measure value generated: *Valuation: Measuring and Managing the Value of Companies*, Wiley, 2005.

not worrying about whether these result from small margins or large. Examples include numerous commodity industries such as those making plastic bags, low-cost tapes, or generic over-the-counter drugs.[9] Others are focused on high-margin profits— profits that also come with high returns on investment. These organizations are willing to compromise on volume to achieve these high returns.

The organization looks to hire you because it believes you can help it make more profits.[10] Thus, your primary role in any company is to make more profits or reduce costs by either developing new products, increasing sales, developing new technologies for new products, or developing new manufacturing processes or improving existing ones. Your role could also be in business development. Alternatively, you might be involved in developing strategies or helping with logistics or administration of the organizations to support growth of profits or cost reductions.

The financial performance and strategy of a company affect how you do your job. They define what aspect of the organization's strategies you implement, how people can count on you, or the nature of your interaction with others. It also defines your work schedule (how flexible can it be—less in a manufacturing job or where people need to interact with you, more if

[9]Some companies can make strategic decisions to stay in commodity businesses that give them large volumes even though margins are low or because it gives them strategic presence in a certain section of the supply chain. This does not mean that they are small companies. Other companies will choose to forgo sections of the market that do not provide significant margins even at the cost of volume; and again, this does not mean they are niche or small companies either. These are strategic decisions that companies make; and as a new employ, it is important to know your companies' strategies so that your solutions and career strategies align with them. Companies may have different strategies for different products or markets.

[10]A bit dated but good review of corporate evaluation of profits: D. C. Miller, *The Dynamics of Company Profits*, Cambridge University Press, 1990.

you primarily work by yourself), the nature of your work (are you developing new products, trouble shooting, developing growth strategies, or managing programs), and thus a significant part of your life. Whether you are growing satisfied with your work and feel fulfilled depends on your role in the organization. Whether you are able to balance your work and life in a way that is satisfying to you also depends on your role in the organization.

And yet, your work can transcend your position. The advantage of being a knowledge worker, beyond (and besides) being a chemist or a physicist or an engineer, is that it lets you transcend your role in the organization. *This is a key aspect in understanding how you can define your industrial career—your primary role is to solve problems.* Your skills are only tools; and to the extent that you want to, you can learn and develop new skills. This view is empowering because you are now not defined by a set of skills or functions that an organization needs. If you understand the organization, you can solve problems that the organization has—you can choose the kinds of problems and the nature of the solutions in ways that are consistent with your values and your life goals. Your career is now defined by what *you* want to do.

The experience of a scientist in a Fortune 100 company exemplifies how empowering this idea can be. This man, an expert in modeling fluids in flow and effect of forces and stress on these fluids, was becoming increasingly frustrated by his immediate management's lack of understanding of the value he brought to his group and to his company. He had supported design of products, helped design processing lines that had resulted in commercialization of successful products, and was highly respected by experts in the company. Yet, he was not promoted for years and had begun to become quite frustrated with his position. He looked outside and while there were offers, he realized that similar situations abound in other companies in that industry as well. In addition, he had a family well-settled—his wife was working in another company in the same city and his children were in middle and high school—and preferred not to move.

He realized, then, that his modeling skills could be used to solve other significant problems in the company as well. While continuing at his old job, he began to solve small problems of financial flows and predict commercialization success, pricing, and planning for a director of another business unit. This helped plan commercialization strategies immensely. Soon, the director got special permission to have this modeling expert directly support commercialization strategies. This expert now works for senior executives and has even had a project for the CEO of this Fortune 100 company. He continues to use his skills and solves problems that influence the direction of the company significantly, having influence over the direction of the company—all without moving out of the company. He just realized that he was empowered to solve problems and he found critical problems that he could solve.

STRATEGIES FOR PROFIT

The second characteristic of a company relates to how it makes profits. The strategies that a company uses to make profits define the identity of the organization, its internal dynamics, how it interacts with the rest of the world, and how events in the world affect it.

BUSINESS MODELS AND YOUR COMPANY

A key component of a company's strategy is its business model[11]: how is it based on their product leadership (including

---

[11]More readings on business models: A. Afuah, *A Strategic Management Approach*, McGraw-Hill/Irwin, 2003.

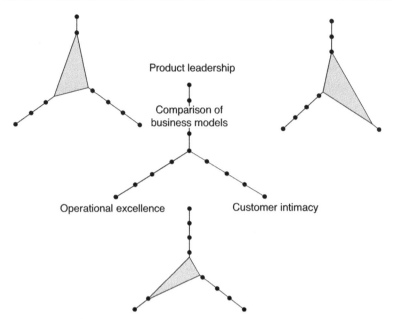

FIGURE 2.1. Comparison of leadership attributes of companies with different business models.

technology innovation,[12] intellectual property, brand), intimacy with customers (including relationship with customers and understanding their needs, customization), and operational excellence (efficiency, price, defining position on value chain). How does your candidate company position itself? If you had 5 points to distribute among these three factors, how would you rate your candidate company (more points imply strong leadership)?

Figure 2.1 shows a schematic of such a company profile tool that provides an indication of the company's business model. The central figure shows the three axes that measure different leadership strengths of a company. The diagrams around it show three examples of companies that are strong in one or another of those leadership attributes. It is natural for a company

[12]R. Burgelman, C. Christensen, and S. Wheelwright, *Strategic Management of Technology and Innovation*, McGraw-Hill/Irwin, 2003.

to be strong in one; in fact, it is important that a company have a dominant strength since it will be driven by that strength. The top left figure shows a company that is driven by leadership in technology or product innovation (e.g., Intel or 3M). The top right shows a company that is strong in customer relationship (such as Disney), while the bottom shows a company whose strength is organizational efficiency (such as Walmart, Aldi).

Traditionally, it was acknowledged that there is no absolute advantage in one business model or the other, though certain models do better in specific markets. However, some recent studies have argued that in the last few decades, companies that are led by operational experience have done better. Irrespective, it is important for a company to have a well-defined leadership strategy: Will the company drive growth through product innovation, operational excellence, or customer intimacy? Of course, a company that leads through product innovation also has to have customer relations and a base level of operational excellence. However, a company that does not define its strategy and attempts to do all things is bound to fail. For one, the growth drivers and its leadership strategy is defined in its organizational structure. A company that is organized for growth through product development will have a strong technology and product development lab with adequate support on sales, marketing, and logistics. If a company with such an organizational structure attempts to lead through marketing, it is bound to fail. (Such a company could attempt to be more effective in sales and marketing to support its product leadership.)

Consider a company that develops robust but hardly innovative products and has very strong customer relationship. The core of that company has to be its organizations that interact with customers: sales, marketing, and customer service. These groups will help the company understand what customers really want through extensive research about customer behavior.

Product plans and details of commercialization will be drawn up based on these studies. The technical community will develop products in support of these plans. The technology or product development community may also be involved in observing the behavior of "test customers" as they spend time interacting with their products, attempting to learn what inventions can be made to help the customers. The technical community will not be inept by any standards, and people will have good careers; however, their work will be closely driven by market needs rather than a more unconstrained mandate for research that a technology-driven group may enjoy. Businesses will not be developed based on a wild invention outside that core/adjacency. Business growth will often be driven by understanding of its core markets and development of a variety of products that can meet customer needs. The company will have proud stories of market analysis that led to millions of dollars in sales or to key inventions—stories of how better market or voice of customer analysis helped it design the product that dominated the market.

Consider a second company that leads through development of new technologies—those that "wow." The core of the organization has to be the R&D community—those who develop new technologies and products. These groups focus on making key inventions and applying new science to develop technologies that can change the ability to do things, and they will have a more free hand in defining these directions. Technology development is often broader than the core or even near adjacency. Growth will be driven by technology differentiation and product development strategies (which may use market data to prioritize development). Since new product growth is based on development of new technologies, the embodiment of the product is defined further down the development process, and detailed customer analysis can happen only later. Sales, marketing, and customer service are organized to help take these new inventions to the marketplace. These are often smaller organizations. The technology and product development community is strong and very influential—it is the core of the company. Most decision making in such a company is in the hands of individuals who were former technology or product developers. The company will have proud stories of inventions that were a decade ahead of their time, or it will have stories of programs based on inventions that were not going anywhere or were asked to be suspended because there was no business justification but continued nevertheless.

Consider a third company that is driven by understanding the supply chain[13] and through efficient and disciplined management of its supply chain. Most companies that succeed in such efforts are not manufacturers. They may not have R&D labs but have technical expertise that is focused on strong testing abilities, understanding of standards and performance, and the ability to share information efficiently and make decisions. Business growth is driven by increased supply chain efficiency and providing service to customers—not by development of new products or new markets. Business growth will be driven by understanding of supply chains in different sectors and different markets and by organizing of those markets around these supply chains. The company will have proud stories of how they were able to dominate the market by better understanding of the supply chain or logistical reorganization to reduce cost to customers.

Companies also strategize based on position within a value chain of a certain market. For example, a certain section of the value chain of a certain product may require very demanding technologies with rapid changes (this will often also be the high-profit section of the value chain) while other parts of the chain

[13]M. H. Hugos, *Essentials of Supply Chain Management*, Wiley, 2006.

may be commoditized. The demanding and rapidly changing technologies are barriers that prevent other companies from participating. If your company provides solutions in this section of the value chain, it will have to constantly attempt to invent new products and technologies while also having high profit margins. This will define the internal structure of the organization, which must be geared toward efficiently inventing and implementing next-generation technologies in a fast-changing marketplace. The semiconductor industry of the last two decades is an example. There is opportunity for significant personal career growth, and the jobs are often high-pressure jobs.

THE MARKETS IT KEEPS

Beyond understanding the past and current financial performance of a company, it is also necessary to understand the core markets of the company and how they align with global forces.

- What products and services form the core of the company? (Core markets are the target of most of its technology and product development and the source of most of its revenue.)
- Does it have one, two, or a few core markets?[14] Is it strong in its core markets or does it focus on many contiguous markets where it is a significant player?
- What are its adjacent markets?[15]
- Is the company focused on consolidating its core or growing its adjacent markets, or both?

[14]C. Zook and J. Allen, *Profts from the Core: Growth Strategy in an Era of Turbulence*, Harvard Business School Press, 2001.

[15]C. Zook, *Beyond the Core: Expand Your Markets Without Abandoning Your Roots*, Harvard Business School Press, 2004.

- Which is the portion of the supply chain that they occupy, and what is the section of the market in which they are strong?

Working for a company with one or two markets as its core is different from a company that participates in half a dozen markets strongly. In one case, the company probably understands those markets very well and has a variety of products designed for them. As a technical employee, your programs are perhaps focused on applications within these well-defined markets. You have institutional understanding of these markets and intuitively know what products and what innovations are needed in the market space—you have a high probability of commercial success. In the other case, the company may have less understanding of diverse markets. The programs may in fact be driven by new technology rather than by a deep understanding of needs and gaps in the market. As a technical employee, you may find the ability to work on a more diverse set of programs. On the other hand, in the absence of an insider understanding of the market, your barrier to entry may be high, and the uncertainty in market understanding could also lead to lower rates of commercial success.

If one or two markets are core to the company but it is not a major player in the market, then you may have to question the business plans and models used by the company or dig deeper. Is it a new company that is growing? Or has it shrunk? Or has it been stagnant? Does the company have strong technologies and intellectual property, or does it have well-entrenched and robust market channels that protect its core?

In addition, it is important to understand the company's position in the market. Often, markets are like pyramids with (a) high volume and low price at the bottom and (b) high margin and smaller volumes at the top. Of course, the high-margin products are premium products that provide some key performance advantages. Is the company a major player in the market? What is its market share? Is the rest of the market fragmented, or is it controlled by one or two players? Where in the pyramid is the company positioned? Is this consistent with the business model and financial goals of the company? For example, if a company is technology-driven, but mainly provides low-cost technically nondifferentiated solutions and commodity products, then there is a clear conflict. This implies that the company is not playing to its strength and that there is bad management (unless of course the company is using this as a strategy to enter a new market or grow into an area where it is not strong).

It is not just the current financial status and strategic plans that tells you about the health of the company. One also needs to understand its past and its direction forward. Questions regarding it growth plans are also important. Does it plan on consolidating its core further? Will it do so by playing to its business model or diversifying its strategies? For example, will it add new products for its core markets? Or if it is a technology-driven company, will it consolidate by strengthening its customer intimacy or repositioning its supply chain? Does it plan to penetrate down or up into the pyramid? If so, what plans does it have? Does it plan to grow into adjacent spaces?

A COMPANY'S STRATEGY AND YOUR JOB

Your role within any company will depend on the company's strategies and business model (and, of course, your own skills). For example, a software expert in a consumer goods industry will primarily be providing support to help make the organization more efficient in processing information or knowledge sharing. On the other hand, a software expert in a company that develops new database management packages will directly drive product growth. The roles of the same skill set in two different organizations are quite different. The kind of problems that are critical to organizations with different strategies will also be different; hence the kind of problems for which the organization will reward you will also differ.

Are there examples of the above-mentioned business models and market strategies among candidate companies you consider? The quality and quantity of publications in peer-reviewed technical journals as well as number of patents will tell you whether the company has a strong technical leadership. So also, reviewing business magazines analysis of your company will provide input on its organizational and market leadership. In addition, analyzing what other companies participating in the market space have been doing also provides much information. The market itself will also help understand whether the company has the right business model for the market. It is difficult, for example, to drive a company with technology leadership to win in a market space for commodity products.

Consider the three business models described earlier. Which of these business models might be most receptive to your skills an interests? In analyzing this, think of your skills broadly. If you plan on continuing in technology or product development and if inventions give you the thrills, then perhaps a business model that is driven by technology is the one you would look for. On the other hand, if you are really interested in business development but enjoy relating to technology, or even enjoy technology management, a business model that is driven by an understanding of customer needs or one that is driven by technology may both be of interest. If you are interested in organizing markets and if you see your technical knowledge as a useful tool, a business model based on organization efficiency might be of interest. Table 2.1 provides examples of entry level position in companies with different business models.

Career trajectories are different in these companies because the functions that make key business decisions and the skills

TABLE 2.1. AN EXAMPLE OF JOB DESCRIPTIONS AT DIFFERENT LEVELS IN COMPANIES WITH DIFFERENT BUSINESS MODELS

	Technology-Driven Growth	Market-Driven Growth	Efficient Organization-Driven Growth
Entry level product developer	Product design for performance significantly *beyond* current standards	Product design to *meet* specific customer needs	Redesign known products to stay outside intellectual property boundaries and *keep cost low*
Senior product developer	Identify areas of new technology/ product development with *new performance attributes*	Work with customer teams to *understand what the market needs* and how it can be provided	Identify new products based on *supply chain and product value proposition*
New manager	Scoping out *new technology opportunities* and mapping technology strategy to grow into adjacent spaces or to consolidate core markets (with market input)	Identifying *technologies that can address specific product requirements* defined by market needs. Develop strong understanding of markets in which the company plays	Scope market for *opportunities to reorganize supply chain*, or build more effective solutions that meet section of customer needs

that influence these decisions are different. Ask yourself what kinds of responsibilities are involved at the next job level and how you can become involved in those responsibilities or at least exposed to them at your current position. Also ask yourself what skills are needed to help you fulfill responsibilities at the next level.

Irrespective of your situation, you need to understand how the company helps you in moving to positions of higher responsibility or leadership. How does it expose you to more challenging problems or provide you with opportunities to learn the skills needed at positions of higher responsibility? This analysis is not just useful for those looking for jobs, but it also presents a development plan for new employees. An understanding of nature of jobs and the strategy of a company can help define your development plan.

In a company like Dow, a large fraction of technical positions are chemists, chemical engineers, or materials scientists. If you are a new employee with a physics or math degree in such a company, the kinds of jobs available to you—and hence the potential paths for growth— are more limited. Perhaps you are a physicist or a biochemist who applies your understanding of physical or biochemical properties of materials to design new materials. It may be worthwhile to begin to learn chemistry or materials science and hence broaden your knowledge base (and potential access to many more positions). This does not have to occur through degrees—often on the job training supplemented by courses taught within the company is sufficient. Having done this opens up many more positions, and hence many more paths for growth open up. Or you could explore the interdisciplinary regime between physics and chemistry—a formula that has been vital to many careers.

A proactive approach to managing your career requires you to understand your company's business model: It tells you what skills and what roles are more important in its processes. This includes an understanding of external trends that are affecting the company and those which the company recognizes as important. Becoming involved in solving problems relevant to these strategies or developing and implementing strategies for the above-mentioned trends could also lead to growth.

Many successful professionals have taken advantage of changing trends to bring increased profits to their organizations and grow along. For example, the fact that there is a growing aging population that needs new solutions to fulfill their needs—whether for independent living, health care, and others—has resulted in new avenues for business growth. Thus, scientists or managers working on sensors have been able to apply these to help solve problems in these areas (new sensors that trigger alarms if someone falls, or if someone has not moved for an extended period, or even sensors that take biological readings and transmit them to some central system). Devices that can help mobility of senior citizens has been another business area. In each case, the fundamental science has been the same but has been applied to key new areas where one expects business growth; and in being able to connect this understanding of business trends with scientific or technical expertise, people have grown in their careers.

What are some growing industries where your skills would bring much value, where you could solve business critical problems? What are one or two skills that would significantly improve your value to high growth industries? Clearly, understanding the business model of your company (or a company of interest) and the trends in the market spaces in which your company participates can help you identify key opportunities. Connecting those with your skills on one hand, and profits for the company on the other, can lead to vehicles for growth—for yourself and maybe for the company.

HOW IS IT ORGANIZED?

In introducing you to companies, we talked about the profit motive and that companies were built around strategies to achieve those profits. We also described how the company was organized to implement the strategies they had set out for themselves. In understanding a company of interest, then, it is important to understand its organization and how it helps or hinders the company's ability to implement its strategies. Is the organizational structure aligned with the strategy? If it is a technology-driven company, does it invest in technology development? Is there a strong core of technologies and technology developers? If it is a company driven by strong customer relationship, is there a strong sales and marketing section? Is the company organized by functions or by markets? How much overlap exists between the sections? Is the company global and is the organization structure global?

We noted that the goal of the company is to make profits and that your job is to understand its strategy and help the company make profits. Understanding the organization helps you to (a) recognize where you are in it and (b) recognize your pathways and access to customers, to organizations making sales, and to resources you need to solve problems. Your position in the organization will help you understand what problems you are being asked to solve—you need to understand how you will effectively implement these solutions based on access and pathways to the customer and to resources. Thus, knowledge about the organization with regard to how it is arranged and how it plans to execute its strategy based on its business model will significantly help define a successful career strategy for an individual.

1. It helps you understand the role of your job or potential job within the strategic plans and roadmap of the organization.

2. It defines strategies that you can use to (a) achieve and build greater profits for the company based on the above understanding or (b) influence decisions.

3. It helps you understand decision-making processes and key business stakeholders and thus shape the strategies for ones own success (and hence impact one's own career growth).

Figure 2.2 shows an organizational strategy where different groups use some common resources to address different sections of the total market space. These common resources are groups such as R&D, Communications, and so on. Examples could include various consumer goods manufacturers—a consumer goods company might be serving a variety of markets

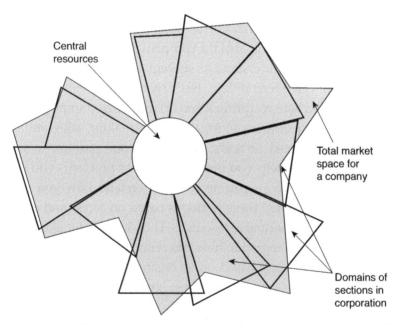

Central resources

Total market space for a company

Domains of sections in corporation

FIGURE 2.2. The total market space is shown by the gray polygon. The bold triangles represent responsibilities of different sections of the corporation; note that there are gaps in the market space that are not addressed by this company, along with areas of overlap.

that do not overlap. Each division of the company might be focused on a specific market. One group may be focused on detergents; another group on ice creams; yet another group on industrial chemicals; a fourth on paints. And yet, all of these might be based on fundamental research on surfactants, colloids, and emulsions.

For any of these structures, the following framework provides useful guidance in thinking through the organizational aspects of the company even though answers to the questions it raises may not be easily available. In understanding the ability of the company to implement its strategic goals, one can define the total market space of the company—current and potential. It then validates how effectively the company is able to address needs in the total market space by asking the following questions:

- Are all parts of the company aligned with a cohesive strategy? What is the underlying theme on which the company is built?

- Is the company structured in a way that prevents overlap and redundancy? Are there sections that conflict or overlap on the value chain? Is one section of the company interacting with customers in a way that undermines another section? Are division roles well-defined and modes of interaction laid out? Does each section own all responsibility for the market it serves?

- Is the company structured in a way that no significant market area is left unaddressed or inaccessible? If there are gaps, are these opportunities for you?

- Is the organization of the company a cause for non-access to certain sections of the value chain?

- Is the company able to ensure that its core strengths are in intimate contact with the market areas? For example, if technology is the core strength of the company, do technology groups understand the markets? And are they developing solutions in strategic but active interaction with the representatives of the market (consumers, channels, etc.)? Similarly, if manufacturing efficiency is the core strength, are these groups in close contact with the markets?

- Are the company's core strengths effectively enabled to provide solutions to the markets? For a company whose core strength is technology development, is customer service infrastructure, or marketing or communications, organized to ensure that the technology group can understand market needs and provide solutions?

Other organizational structures also exist (see Figures 2.3 and 2.4). In each case, your role strategies and growth plans will be different.

In understanding the organization of a company and its implication on your career, you have to study the overall strategy of the company and its organizational structure as well as that of the specific group you join. The former is the framework of how you might grow or the constraints to your growth. The latter provides you with an understanding of your immediate job, what you need to succeed now, and possible paths from here on.

Irrespective of the structure of an organization, functional efforts are based on a network of roles that collaborate, communicate, and sometimes overlap to implement the strategies for the vision and mission of the organization (see Figure 2.5). As you work on any project, your role leverages your local and global organization. You will have to connect with members who have more or less at stake in the project. At the same time, you will have to influence key decision makers. How you do this successfully is critically dependent on the organizational structure and your understanding of it.

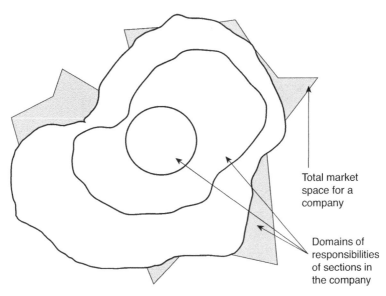

Total market
space for a
company

Domains of
responsibilities
of sections in
the company

FIGURE 2.3. The total market space is shown by the gray polygon. The company is organized into sections that are vertically integrated, where the output of one becomes the input of the second. Such companies may show a certain extent of vertical integration where they choose to develop various aspects of the supply chain by themselves. Some automobile companies would be examples of this kind of organization, where each organization would develop several components of the vehicle. Organizations could also be structured as hybrids of the above examples.

Figure 2.5 provides a schematic of such a workspace with shared responsibilities. It shows the group wholly responsible for the problem, along with its interactions with other groups that may be more or less involved—even groups that perhaps play consulting roles. Even more complex: These groups may lie inside or outside the company.

What is your responsibility in your position and the responsibility of your group? How do these align with the responsibilities of your section? Is your section directly responsible for sales or developing products, or does it play an enabling role? If it is the latter, then you will continue to be *in support* of logistics to drive growth—never in a position to drive growth yourself. You need to clearly recognize this and

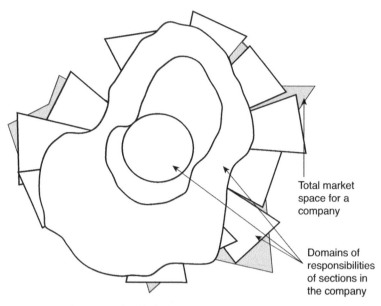

Total market
space for a
company

Domains of
responsibilities
of sections in
the company

FIGURE 2.4. An example of a hybrid organization where tools or products developed by a vertically integrated set of divisions are modified by a market facing divisions for their own markets. The company might serve one large market and thus would have one division providing the final set of solutions to the entire market but have numerous other divisions providing it with a set of input to do so. Automotive companies might be structured this way as well.

analyze how it fits with your career plans. If you would like to drive growth, you would need to find paths to positions within your company or outside that can provide such opportunities. Consider skill development opportunities to do so.

If your section is responsible for sales or developing products, then again consider the impact of your job. For example, is your responsibility aligned with sales into one or a number of market spaces? In that case, look at the total market space and consider how you could either grow your company's market size by identifying new opportunities (and hence influence your own growth) or reduce costs to improve efficiency and profits. The tactics of implementing your strategy will obviously depend on the specificity of your position: Consider who you

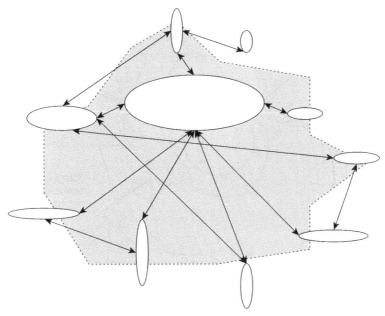

FIGURE 2.5. Schematic of collaboration through a cross organizational network.

might collaborate with and how you could influence decisions in these market spaces and develop a plan to do so.

We remind ourselves that an individual role in a company is to help increase profits for the company and drive growth. Thus the critical question is, What can you do to help the company grow? Your position in the company affects what you can and cannot influence. Your own goals and life need to define what you may want or not want to influence. Your career strategies need to be drawn up based on this understanding.

Organizational efficiency is another aspect of an organization. It reflects the ability of the organization to make decisions based on external stimulus or new internal information. It also provides signs of how easily an individual at different positions (as shown in Figure 2.6) can attempt to promote growth. The organizational efficiency of a company can affect your performance in the company. In knowing how and where decisions

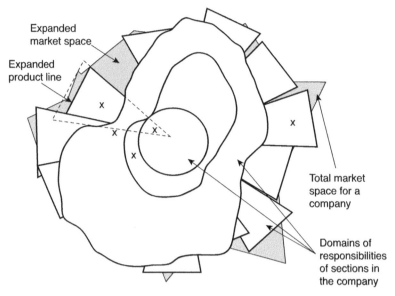

Expanded
market space

Expanded
product line

Total market
space for a
company

Domains of
responsibilities
of sections in
the company

FIGURE 2.6. Your position in the organization affects how you can influence and deliver results. In this figure, locate your position in the company (one of the ×'s). Is yours a growth, consolidation, maintenance, or enabling role? How you would attempt to influence market growth under these different situations?

are made, you have the opportunity to build relationships so that you could have decision makers hear your perspectives. It also sets your expectations and could suggest changes in your career strategies. A less process-oriented organization could lead to much frustration if you expect or work best with well-laid-out processes. It could also slow down processes or get the group mired in major personnel conflicts. However, if it is only somewhat inefficient, it could be a place for much greater freedom in the direction of work or individual choices—this is often true in research labs. It could also result in greater opportunity for a new employee to become involved in decision-making processes and take on leadership roles.

The organization is a living entity, not just branches in a chart. One has to look closely and understand the role of key stakeholders, which may not be obvious from the chart or a listing of "number of people reporting." Other aspects, such as access to key growth areas or markets or even the culture of an organization, are important. For example, a manager leading 40 customer service representatives may look important on an organization chart; but perhaps, depending on the strategy and culture of an organization, it is the group of 10 product developers or maybe 5 marketing personnel who hold the key to critical decisions. Similarly, two groups of developers working on different projects may have changing influence, depending on the trajectory of the company. One has to be aware of the ascent and descent of groups within the organization. This is another facet of the nonlinear nature that organizational dynamics brings to industrial problems.

The evolution of Six Sigma[16] presents an interesting example of the dynamic nature of organizational charts. Numerous companies saw the rise, stagnation, and fall of Six Sigma as a corporate culture. In a number of such companies, since the rise of Six Sigma, many groups had Black Belts (strategic advisers to the group who had no people reporting to them but made key decisions and facilitated direction of programs). During the heyday of Six Sigma, these individuals wielded much influence and were key stakeholders in program directions, even though an organizational chart would show them as a lone individual sitting on a branch with no influence. Since the de-emphasis of Six Sigma, the situation has changed: While the organizational charts in many companies still show this position, their influence has been significantly downgraded. Thus, it is, important to understand the culture and context of a company in understanding the organization.

A JOB IN CHAOS

The complexity of functions and decision-making processes differentiates technical roles in industry from academia. In most cases, key problems in academia (especially for a

---

[16]Six Sigma is a registered servicemark and trademark of Motorola, Inc.

student) involve linear, or perhaps nonlinear, aspects. In the industry, a new graduate will quickly find that decision processes often deal with problems that are nonlinear, if not indeterminate. He or she will also realize that unless one recognizes the difference in the nature of the problem, attempted solutions cause more problems than they resolve.

Linear or simple processes are those where the output that results is proportional to the input and any change in input results in a commensurate change in output. The output of a linear process may be dependent on many parameters (or inputs), but the relationship is with each input separately and in an additive fashion.

Generally, administrative functions are linear. You need to fill out time sheets, report your own equipment inventory, or fulfill certain logistical responsibilities of your group that you may have taken on. There are technical jobs that are also linear. If you do not clean your equipment, your results will be unpredictable.

Nonlinear or complicated processes are ones where the output is dependent on one or many inputs in a way where change in input causes an exponential change in output. In addition, the effect of each input on the output may not be additive. Like linear processes, however, if one understands the nonlinear process, the output is determinate. One right answer exists and one just needs more understanding and sophisticated methods to get there.

Design of a high-performing car might be an example. There are a number of parameters that one can play around with, and the relationships are so tangled that it is not clear how a change in one parameter will affect the final performance. However, it is possible to know the relations. If the understanding of the relationships is well-developed and sophisticated tools are available, multiple solutions can be found and an optimal solution for specific conditions can be predicted.

Complex processes are ones where the components in the system are highly interrelated (it may even be impossible to isolate all the components) as well as dynamic. As a result, there are no right answers and no stable equilibrium states. Most organizations can be described by complex processes: Each group is dynamic, and the relationships between groups are changing and cannot always be described. In fact, understanding of these relationships is not based on predictive equations but on understanding patterns.

Commercialization processes for new products is often a complex process. There are numerous aspects that lead to the complexity: relationships between the technical components, between logistics (raw materials, supplies, equipment), and between organizations and markets. These relationships are constantly changing. One can never expect the nature of a perturbation in these components or predict the best way to respond to these perturbations *a priori*. Thus, experts find solutions by recognizing patterns in the problem—either from their own experience or from those of others—as well as in knowing enough about the techniques that they can access adjacent knowledge and letting solutions emerge.

Heuristically, one can present some guidelines as to whether a certain product has a high or low probability of success. These guidelines could be based on whether similar products exist, whether there has been success in commercialization into similar markets, whether there are major technology hurdles, and so on. However, there are many uncertainties. In addition, many other external aspects also play a big role. For example, a certain product was conceptualized and close to production when there was an unexpected shortage of a key raw material resulting in sudden rise in costs that made the product commercially nonviable. The commercialization plan was shelved. Within months the shortage was over; raw material prices fell back, but the product stayed shelved. Clearly, the timing of the product made a difference. Starting the project 2 months earlier or 6 months later would have led to a different result.

There are also processes (often described as chaotic processes) that are intrinsically indeterminate: We cannot ascertain the output based on the inputs or its initial conditions. It is also impossible to ascertain which of the inputs led to the output. The cause–effect relationships are unclear. This is not because we do not understand the components or the relationships; however, the relationships become so tangled that we cannot know the cause–effect relationships.

For example, whether two groups will have a conflict and how they will resolve it are indeterminate problems. The only way one will know is by having them interact. What strategies will be effective in resolving conflicts will then have to evolve from the nature of their interactions.

Obviously, solutions to these different kinds of problems are different; even approaches to solving these problems will be different. Similarly, responses to these different kinds of processes have to be different. It is thus imperative that a student or a manager of industrial or economic processes acknowledge and recognize these differences; otherwise, managing these problems could result in major failures.

It is important to correctly understand the complexity of a problem. If understood incorrectly, inappropriate strategies would lead to worsening of the problem—and one can find hundreds of such examples in political or organizational case studies. As a trivial example, consider a quadratic equation $x^2 = 4$. If one does not recognize that this is a quadratic equation that can have two roots, then one quickly sees the first solution ($x = +2$) and concludes that the problem is solved. When the problem (or an industrial process) raises other solutions ($x = -2$), the individual does not have the wherewithal to deal with it and takes ineffective measures by either assuming that the process is incorrect or ignoring those solutions or a mixture of these (which often have major implications in real-life situations). It is only *on realizing that the nature of the problem is different and multiple solutions are possible that a student (or a manager of industrial processes) can understand the implications of this other solution and the richness of opportunities that this may bring. (This is true in life as well, but that is a different discussion and can lead to a rich understanding of diversity.)*

In Table 2.2, Snowden and Boone[17] present different sets of strategies to address different kinds of problems.[18]

Your work, success, and impact is dependent on your interactions with and the perspectives and motivations of your boss, your team, and your collaborators—often with multiple functions and perspectives including possibly R&D, product development, quality, business development, and so on. Support from managers of all these collaborators will also impact your success. External factors that lie outside your control or that of the team—for example, raw material costs, other indirect costs, IP issues, and the short- and medium-term direction of and directives within the company (like budget cuts, hiring freeze, etc.)—also influence the success of your work.

[17]D. F. Snowden and M. E. Boone, A leaders framework for decision making, *Harvard Business Review*, November 2007.

[18]It is absolutely necessary to recognize the correct complexity of a process. Albert Einstein is supposed to have said "A scientific theory should be as simple as possible, but no simpler." If you have a "problem" instead of a "scientific theory," it's easier to see that too simple a solution leaves parts of the problem unsolved. And a solution that's not simple enough risks errors (from overcomplication) and consumes resources that could have been better used (attributed to a statement of a monk named William of Occam in the 13th century). Larry Wall, the inventor of the PERL script, said "Using a simple tool to solve a complex problem does not result in a simple solution." This is not to discourage development of simpler models. Even if one were to use a simplifying model, one has to clearly understand the nature of a process and the impact of the simplification. (for example, one could simplify $4 = 2x + 0.01x^2$ as a linear model $4 = 2x$ only when one knows the conditions when the simplification works).

TABLE 2.2. DIFFERENT SETS OF STRATEGIES TO ADDRESS DIFFERENT KINDS OF PROBLEMS

Nature of Problems	Appropriate Strategy
Simple problems	*Sense, Categorize, Respond*: Assess the components of the problem, recognize known and linear relationships, and respond based on understanding of these relationships. Understanding of best practices is useful.
Complicated problems	*Sense, Analyze, Respond*: Assess the components of the problem, analyze and draw conclusions about new components or multiple relationships, and respond based on this understanding. Expertise of nature of components or relationships between components is necessary.
Complex problems	*Probe, Sense, Respond*: Identify the components that are relevant or significant to the problem, recognize the patterns that evolve with respect to the nature of the components and relationships between them, and respond based on evolving understanding. Communication and understanding of dynamic patters is necessary
Chaotic problems	*Act, Sense, Respond*: Act based on limited information, use the response to understand significant components and evolving relationships between components, and develop better response based on this understanding. Dynamic strategy development that includes flexibility of action and expertise in related areas is useful.

In addition, factors completely outside your control such as global events (wars, natural disasters affecting suppliers, etc.), social or economic trends (such as growing older population, increased health-care costs, the onset of recession or rising costs), action by competition (acquisition or mergers, launch of a similar product, bankruptcy), and external R&D (a major discovery, perhaps) may also have a major impact on the success of your work.

Sometimes it is difficult to *a priori* recognize the nature of the problem. Work done (R&D) to solve some well-defined problems is also linear (though the problem itself may be nonlinear or even chaotic—what this means is that the result or the impact of solving the problem is linear, well-defined, and determinate). For example, you might be assigned to develop a code that will simulate a specific system. Or you may be asked to synthesize a specific molecule with a specific structure. Synthesizing this molecule or developing the code could be a difficult problem that requires you to explore different methods or even push science and make inventions—but given that this is a closed, well-defined problem, the impact of your solving this problem is linear, especially when the request for R&D is closely tied to a product.

Often, there are problems whose impact depends on the method or nature of solution. In a school setting, this impact is not relevant because you get a paper or even a patent in solving it. In an industrial setting, the method or process of solution defines whether you can practice it or not (from an intellectual property perspective or from a regulation or environmental perspective, or whether the method gives rise to by-products that are unwieldy), whether it is economically feasible or not, whether it impacts other products or gives rise to other technologies or not, or whether it has strategic value for your company, for competition, or for customers. Sometimes, the identity and role of your collaborators can impact the commercial success of your project. These considerations can bring in nonlinear or chaotic components to your role.

Another set of functions that are truly chaotic or nonlinear are ones that require you to scope and define problems or to make organizational or strategic decisions for the company. For example, should your company be a participant in health-care markets and, if so, what would be your product or service? Or even the more mundane problem of choosing suppliers—what is their position in the supply chain, for example?—can be a complex problem. Similarly, other problems of how to organize the company, what kinds of collaborations to form, or which section of the supply chain to focus are all examples of nonlinear or chaotic processes.

Entry-level positions will require limited exposure to problems of complicated or complex nature. However, your ability to take on and resolve more complicated and chaotic problems is evidence to your management about your leadership skills and your potential to grow. In essence, growth is based on your developing skills to effectively address increasingly nonlinear and chaotic problems.

CULTURE OF THE ORGANIZATION

From a career perspective, the culture of a company—and of your group within the company—plays an important role. It affects your plans of work–life balance as well as your career aspirations. A young scientist with very aggressive career plans joined a company known to be conservative about risks and business choices. He chose to advance an area that the company had dabbled in but had time and again shied away from—the area was a high-risk, high-reward one. He not only was successful in developing prototypes and advancing the technology in the area but also managed to convince senior technical experts to collaborate with him in developing an active team. However, despite these successes, middle management refused to support the program or commit to participating in this market. Frustrated, this very high-achieving and capable young scientist left this company for another company. Clearly, the culture did not match with the interests and aspirations of this young professional. (Hopefully, this young professional thought through the strategies and the culture of the new company he joined.) On the other hand, such a scenario might be an appropriate place for individuals who consider their profession as an effective way to make a good livelihood so that they can have a good quality of life (and this does not mean they are not diligent).

Culture is the DNA of a company.[19] It provides the blueprint of how an organization celebrates, attacks, defends, acts under pressure, or fights back. It is perhaps the most important component of an organization, and yet it is the most difficult to describe. The organization of a company may change, its CEOs may change, and even its product lines and core competencies may change, but the culture of an organization is most enduring. It changes over time—yes. But of all the characteristics of a company, it is most enduring. Hence, in trying to understand any company, it is most important to understand its culture. And yet, it is the most difficult to grasp.

The significance of the culture of a company is perhaps most obvious when two companies merge or when a company ac-quires another—there are often conflicts and difficulties. Diffe-rences in cultures are a major reason why many mergers and acquisitions struggle to succeed. This is perhaps the biggest reason that one should understand the culture of a company where one wants to work—if one is not comfortable with the culture of the company, one will most likely not be successful.

The culture of a company is like the personality of an individual. It is a collection of said and unsaid rules by which all people in a company act. It includes the values of a company. It is embodied in every employee and in their day-to-day action. It is how people interact with each other. For example, one scientist mentioned that in his company, sharing of knowledge is expected and is the norm. Individuals who do not do so are often looked down upon by peers. Culture is the net bias that

---

[19] A basic book on corporate cultures, describing how they evolve and impact on careers, is: T. Deal and A. Kennedy, *Corporate Cultures: The Rites and Rituals of Corporate Life*, Basic Books, 2000. There are numerous other books on this subject, but this is a good book to begin.

people have in making choices—how employees act with respect to other party intellectual property or their own, how employees act regarding hazards and environmental safety, and how employees react to crisis. Essentially, the culture of a company describes how the company attempts to influence entities inside its organization as well as forces external to it (to the extent that it can) to continue to be successful.

Toyota values its employees. Even in the 1990s, under immense pressure from analysts to reduce costs, the president of Toyota clearly directed that while costs had to be reduced, no jobs could be cut. Even in 2008, Autoblog—a webmagazine focused on the automotive industry—published this:

> Toyota is struggling to sell trucks and SUVs like everyone else, but unlike the competition, no full-time workers from stalled factories are getting laid off. The 4,500 workers at idled plants are instead bettering themselves through education by taking classes on safety, diversity, and Toyota history. They're also doing community service while on the clock and even some gardening. The workers will be learning how to work faster and smarter during the down time, and are even being shifted to busier plants on a temporary basis to help plants that are working beyond capacity to keep up with demand.

> Toyota's plan to keep its workers busy at all costs isn't cheap, as about $50 million is being spent to keep workers busy with training programs. Of course, you can't please everyone and the plan isn't sitting well with all of Toyota's workforce, as workers at running factories don't like the fact that laid off workers are getting a leg up on training. A more skilled plant could have an advantage over others in getting earmarked for future products, so unaffected workers also want the extra training.

Toyota commits itself to the no-layoff policy. Fujio Cho, chairman of Toyota Motor Corporation, says:

> Many good American companies have respect for individuals and practice kaizen and other TPS tools. But what is important is having all elements together as a system. It must be practiced every day in a very consistent matter—not in spurts—in a concrete way on the shop floor.

That defines the culture at Toyota.

Groups within a large company will also have subcultures. These will usually be variations to the culture of the company. In some cases it may also deviate from the culture of the company itself. The subculture of the group is as important as the culture of the company, and a candidate for a position or a new employee must recognize the details of the culture and how it impacts his job and career.

Culture can be described to be made up of methods that the company has found most effective in achieving its strategy. It is perhaps a legacy of best practices built over years. It will thus be found in stories and legends that are passed down during group meetings and informal lunches, award ceremonies, and picnics, and the morals will be essentialized and celebrated in these legends. In fact, a vice president of a large company, in discussing new employee orientation processes, pointed out that as a large number of people leave the company through retirement, the legends and oral histories that are lost are as important as the details of experiences in solving various problems. He then suggested that new employees need to be exposed to these stories—they carry the essence of the culture, the meme[20] that defines the organization.

Often, a company will put together guidelines or set up reward systems to build a certain kind of culture. A large agrochemical MNC, for example, has set up a reward system to ensure strong and proactive development of its employees—technical, personal, and leadership development. The reward system is set up such that 50% of any manager or group leader's appraisal depends on his or her team's development. This ensures that every manager is looking out for ways to help his or her team develop—gain new technical skills, take on

[20]Richard Dawkins, *The Selfish Gene*, Oxford University Press, 2006.

leadership opportunities, avail of mentoring or coaching opportunities or learn various social, collaborative, conflict resolution, or other "soft skills" constantly.

This ensures that employees continue to grow and learn on the job. Employees know that their managers are looking out for them to help their growth. At the same time, this culture also ensures that the company is developing leadership inside its organization.

That is not to say that all cultural aspects of a company are appropriate or effective. Given that they are made of legends and are bundles of tradition, they may include aspects that may be anachronistic—leftovers of gender or racial discrimination perhaps. Or they could include technical or management practices that were perhaps appropriate in the slower-moving world of the 1970s and 1980s but not in the globalized and faster moving world today. It is important to recognize the culture of a company and ask whether it is appropriate in today's world and consistent with one's own values and needs.

Of course, cultures change. Usually they change slowly, responding to the changes in the world. Sometimes they change rapidly, responding to strong direction by a CEO or President. However, they change slowly enough that an employee should consider it as a significant influence on his or her career.

How a company helps you learn its work environment of the company, shares the cultural components that help you be successful, coaches you in understanding details and nuances that are the difference between a successful project and a failed one, treats you when you succeed and when you don't, accepts your new ideas or radically different suggestions, and treats you when it has to let you go are all part of the culture. The culture influences all other parameters we have discussed thus far. Hence, it should be a key aspect you consider in analyzing a company and if it is right for you.

An Environment for Growth

The environment that is fostered by a culture of a company will affect the new employee most because a new employee is taking his or her first steps, with his or her potential infinite. The process of growing within a company means two things:

1. You will try new solutions. How open is the company culture to accepting new ideas?
2. You will make mistakes. How does the company react to your making mistakes and how does it hold you accountable?

You will attempt to take on more responsibilities and make dynamic decisions on problems that are unknown and unknowable until you begin to work on them. This is the only way the company can grow. In doing so, however, you will also propose solutions or make recommendations that may be different from how the organization has operated so far, or perhaps radically new and hence risky. You should find out how the organization deals with new ideas. Can you or someone else in the company identify what these new ideas have been and how the company may be acting radically differently now than it did 10 years ago?

The answer to this question will often help you gauge how open the company may be to new ideas. There have been major technology developments in the last decade, making what may not have been technically or economically feasible then, practical today. The environment within which a company attempts to make profits is changing—how is the company willing to adapt its business model, its operations, and its technological solutions in a concerted fashion to continue to make profits or even grow in this dynamic environment?

You also need to recognize that different industries react differently and that what may be a good strategy in one

industry may not be a good one in another. While the IT or
finance industries have been proactive in implementing new
strategies, some chemical companies have been less so. New
ways of thinking or new solutions may have been more con-
strained by the business environment, simply because it was
unfeasible to attempt large-scale changes in such a large and
slow business. Cell-phone companies will be more willing to try
new ideas than will oil-refining companies.

It is also important to note that some organizations are so
blown away by radically new ideas that they are unwilling to
go through the same kind of due diligence that any other
idea would have to. Thus, the processes that helped ensure
that an idea was truly a good one, irrespective of whether it is
radical or a traditional solution, were abandoned. The processes that could have helped the radical idea evolve through
addressing key critical concerns were ignored. The idea then
is doomed to fail despite itself; this is a result of poor all
around management as well as bad implementation of
the idea.

A complementary question to the above discussion is
around the organizations appetite to accept honest failures. If
you are trying out new solutions—and that is always
necessary when you are exploring complex and revolutionary
problems—you will make mistakes. How does the company
react to such mistakes or failures? Are you held accountable,
and in what way? It is important that you be held accountable
because your mistake could have affected others in your organization. Not holding you accountable means that there is no
difference whether you succeed or not, and that would affect
the morale and effectiveness of the company. At the same time,
the process of holding you accountability must also ensure that
you are not so badly affected that you are unwilling to try other
new ideas. Accountability is not based on your being radical
and implementing new ideas but on the diligence of the

implementation and analysis and implication of these ideas (which must also be the "touchstone" for nonradical solutions).

In this context it is useful to present the McKnight Principle[21]—one that defines 3M's employee culture. The following is from 3M's website:

> William L. McKnight joined Minnesota Mining and Manufacturing Co. in 1907 as an assistant bookkeeper. He quickly rose through the company, becoming president in 1929 and chairman of the board in 1949.
>
> Many believe McKnight's greatest contribution was as a business philosopher, since he created a corporate culture that encourages employee initiative and innovation.
>
> His basic rule of management was laid out in 1948:
>
> "As our business grows, it becomes increasingly necessary to delegate responsibility and to encourage men and women to exercise their initiative. This requires considerable tolerance. Those men and women, to whom we delegate authority and responsibility, if they are good people, are going to want to do their jobs in their own way.
>
> Mistakes will be made. But if a person is essentially right, the mistakes he or she makes are not as serious in the long run as the mistakes management will make if it undertakes to tell those in authority exactly how they must do their jobs.
>
> Management that is destructively critical when mistakes are made kills initiative. And it's essential that we have many people with initiative if we are to continue to grow."

SUMMARY

Most technology companies can be described by the parameters described above, and there is overlap between those

---

[21]http://solutions.3m.com/wps/portal/3M/en_US/our/company/information/history/McKnight-principles/.

parameters. What seems missing in the above description is any judgment of a company along these parameters: Is a company that is aggressive with personnel better than one that is not? Is one that is aggressive in marketing better than one that is innovative in technology? Is one that is focused on few core competencies better than one that is more diversified?

Unfortunately, there are no clear answers, though business analysts have attempted to use statistics and heuristics to argue one way or the other. Irrespective, the question needs to be reframed: What kind of company will be a better match for you? There is no clear answer; it depends on your personality, your leanings, your phase of life, your interests, and your ambitions.[22]

This is not a recipe to rate companies in an objective manner; there is no such method. This is an attempt to sketch organizations based on some key characteristics of any economic venture. The next chapter will be an attempt to help you understand your own leanings and needs and guidelines for you to explore whether your needs and personality align with the nature, goals, and strategy of a given company or organization.

KEY TAKEAWAYS

1. It is necessary to understand the key goals of an organization—the kind of profits it makes, the strategies it uses to make profits, and the organizational structure it embodies to implement these strategies. Your job will be strongly affected by these aspects. Your ability to deliver and be successful will also depend on these.

[22]Despite the popular misconception that without formal MBA degrees, individuals can only go so far, numerous current and recent CEOs in large companies have been technically trained; Dow, 3M, Intel, GE, and AMD are all examples.

Hence, it is important that even as a new employee you recognize these aspects of your company.

2. Your primary goal is to help your company make profits. Your success will usually depend on your effectiveness in achieving this. Your skills are only your tools; they should aid you in achieving your goals, not constrain you in what you can or cannot do. Thus, it is up to you to scope and solve key problems for your organization, irrespective of your degree or your job description.

3. It is important to understand clearly your company's strategy to make profits. Is the company's dominant strategy based on technology development, strong customer understanding, or operations development? Also understand its key markets and its supply chain and value proposition within these markets. These will often direct the goals of your job, what solutions will be successful, and what projects will be important to your company; thus it will define your job as well the trajectory for career growth.

4. How is the company organized to face its markets? And where are you in the organizational structure? Is your role enabling or driving commercialization? Answers to these questions help you understand your sphere of influence as well as identify key stakeholders in the decision-making process. It also helps you plan your career.

5. Understand that the nature of problems you face can be different, and potential solution strategies will have to be commensurately different. Learn how you can recognize linear, nonlinear, and complex or chaotic processes. Your ability to take on and resolve more complicated and chaotic problems is evidence to your management about your leadership skills and your

potential to grow. Growth is based on your developing skills to effectively address increasingly nonlinear and chaotic problems.

6. What are your strengths and weaknesses in solving different kinds of problems? With what kinds of problems have you had the most experience? To what kinds of problems do you need more exposure?

7. Culture is the DNA of a company. If one is not comfortable with the culture of the company, one will most likely not be successful. Thus, culture of your company impacts your performance in the company. Culture influences all other parameters we have discussed thus far. Hence, it should be a key aspect you consider in analyzing a company and if it is right for you.

8. Identify the salient characteristics of the culture of a company and understand what they mean to you? How do they connect with your values? Where are they aligned, and are there aspects that bother you?

9. Recognize that your growth in the company depends on you taking on new problems and providing new solutions. Understand how the company deals with new ideas and how it responds to successes and to failures. Is it an innovative company, a company willing to take risks or a conservative company? What processes does it have to explore and screen new efforts. Understand how it will help you succeed and how it will hold you accountable. This should influence your solution strategies as well as help you manage expectations with key stakeholders.

10. How can you describe various companies of interest by the framework described above and be able to extrapolate what they may mean to your skills, interests, and career?

CHAPTER

3

THE PROTAGONIST OF YOUR CAREER

Who are you and what do you want? This is not an essay in existentialism but instead an attempt to understand what you want from your career, its significance in your life, and how it can be fulfilling—perhaps the most important criteria in a "successful career." Even at the cost of repetitiveness, it is worth pointing out that this book is not a recipe book for getting promotions. Such a recipe book does not exist, and any attempt to write one is an oversimplification of both the workplace and people. (A "successful" career for one person may be stressful for another and may be an unbalanced life for a third.) Instead, this is an exercise in self-analysis to understand what choices one has within the framework of industrial jobs (as described earlier) and how they may or may not align with ones own skills, personality, and needs. Hence, one has to begin by understanding ones own needs, personality, strengths, and weaknesses.

Planning a Scientific Career in Industry: Strategies for Graduates and Academics
By Sanat Mohanty and Ranjana Ghosh
Copyright © 2010 John Wiley & Sons, Inc.

DREAMS AND YOUR JOB

Take a moment to create a list of things most important to you in your life. Perhaps these include your relationship with you spouse and children, your hobbies or your progress in work, how much money you earn, or how much leisure time you have. You may even want to prioritize these. Recognize the value of these components in your life and how your job might affect them. If you make career choices (often subconsciously or under pressure) where your schedules and priorities do not align with what you care about, you will be frustrated.

Even as you put this together, you know that these goals and this wish list will change. In changing, they reflect that you change and that you grow. And as your goals and your equilibrium in work–life balance change, so will your priorities. At any time, however, you need to recognize how your work and career plans are aligned to achieve this balance. You could choose to deviate from it, but it should be a conscious choice based on (a) an understanding of where you would ideally like this balance to be and (b) a plan of what you get by deviating from it for a certain length of time.

For example, while your life equilibrium may require you to spend time with your family, your work may require you to travel or stay away for long stretches of time. This should be a conscious decision based knowing that there are needs you are not fulfilling today so that you could make career or financial gains in the short term leading to better equilibrium in the long term. If not, either your equilibrium will shift (you will realize that you really want to be a high career achiever) or there will be frustration.

Such introspection does not tell you what you can and cannot do or what you should and should not do. It only provides the basis for you to know yourself and help you decide what you would like as an ideal career. A successful career for you cannot then be defined by a standardized metric of money, fame, power, or another such parameter. A successful career for you is one that is closely aligned with your ideal career (or consistent with your life equilibrium) *at any time*.

The presence of other activities or growth components in your life does not mean that you cannot or should not be aggressive or ambitions with regard to your career. It means that you should do everything you can with regard your career but balance it so that you are doing everything you want to with your family and other components of your life. It should help remind you that not achieving all your career goals in the way you have set them out and in the time frame you chose does not imply a failed life. In fact, often, your involvement in other things and your success in them (as a parent or spouse, as an active community member, etc.) can give you strength to make more bold career moves and feel secure to take steps that you may not otherwise.

BUILDING ON YOUR SKILLS

Having recognized your own life balance, there is a need to know your skills, your personality, and your values. Enumerating your skills should be easy. Your resume should be a statement of your skills. While this book is not a primer for resume writing,[23] it is important to think about your skill set in the context of what industries want. Industries want to make profits using strategies they have chosen and with an organizational structure designed to implement those strategies. How do your skills align with the strategies of the industry, how can you help them make profits, and where in the organization would you fit? These should be answered by your resume.

---

[23]A good example is a 2007 McGraw-Hill publication entitled *Resumes for Scientific and Technical Careers* by McGraw-Hill editors.

In thinking about your skills, then, you cannot be too broad and vague or too narrow.

Often a candidate will define her/his experience in great detail but very narrowly. Let us look at our sample candidate's description of her experience: "Understanding the folding of a very specific protein molecule in specific solvents under specific conditions of pH and salt concentration." She will then describe the tools with which she has expertise or is acquainted. It is often up to the interviewer (if the candidate gets that far) to then understand what this candidate has to offer to the company and how her skills are relevant, especially if the area of research is not of direct interest to the company. If this candidate looked at her skills vis-à-vis how they brought value to the company of interest, perhaps she might be able to show the relevance of her skills to this company more directly.

Companies have to hire for specific positions. In most groups (within any company), hiring opportunities are few and far between. While theoretically, all good managers will agree that the best person needs to be hired irrespective of specific skills match, given the pressures today, managers are also looking for the new hire to get on to solving problems quickly, which implies that the initial learning time is not as long as it used to be. Thus, managers will often hire a strong candidate who has skills relevant to the position over an excellent candidate who may have had major inventions but whose area of expertise is different. At the same time, managers are also aware that it is rare that a person spends the rest of his or her career in the same area of expertise. With changing economic pressures, companies often dynamically emphasize and deemphasize programs. A candidate with diversity in experience or one who can show that she can solve a wide set of problems is of high value: It means that this candidate can easily move across projects as demanded and solve new kinds of problems in areas outside of her domain of expertise. This knowledge can help a candidate think about her skills with greater consciousness and present them with more savvy.

Let us consider that a student who worked on the above-mentioned problem of protein folding is considering a position in a non-biofocused chemical company. A typical resume of an individual with such an experience will usually find little interest in a non-biofocused company. After all, how many paint industries care about protein folding, or how many lubricant manufacturers care about association of biomolecules? As an exercise, we will attempt to rewrite her resume in a way that will share how her expertise is of relevance to such a company (without attempting to pad her resume in any way).

- *Experience*: Understanding how thermodynamics affects the interaction of macromolecules (especially biomolecules) as a function of solvent conditions and prediction of properties of these systems under different conditions.

- *Tools and Expertise*: Formulation of macromolecular dispersions. Various characterization techniques (x-ray, light scattering, NMR, chromatography). Modeling of macromolecules using molecular dynamics methods.

- *Skills*: Structure–property of macromolecules, charge interactions, biomolecular properties, design of materials based on macromolecular structure properties, surface and bulk properties of macromolecular dispersions.

- *Value to the Company*: (How does this experience and these tools bring value to a company? What are different roles in this company's organization where her skills would bring value? Which strategies can she affect?) Can design systems that require controlled dispersion or coagulation of macromolecules or particles—of use in design of syrups, gels, composites, foams used in various materials industries (paints, adhesives, plastic composites), and pharmaceutical formulations, as well as in separation industry. Can analyze or test systems for the quality of dispersion or for design flaws. Can design formulations (paints, adhesives, syrups) for specific interactions with surfaces of interest.

The exercise above focused only on technical skills but clearly showed how skills and experiences should be articulated to be meaningful to the targeted company. It has taken a narrowly written resume and attempted to discover the core skills that were learned in that experience. It then shows how those skills are relevant to another industry. This is not an exercise in padding her resume or adding false information. It is an exercise that describes to a company how this student's skills are relevant to their industry and what problems she can help them solve. But this also requires that she truly understand her core skills (beyond being able to describe her project) and connect how those skills impact a different industry. Thus, her experience with protein folding could imply that she really understands the behavior of charged particles in solvents, or that she can analyze various components to predict how such systems would behave. Now this experience is significantly more broadly applicable and can be used not only in protein systems in pharmaceutical industries but also for other entities (like charged particles and other organic molecules). Without such an analysis, she only focused on specific kinds of pharmaceutical companies; other companies would have to abstract this from her interview with them (if she got that far).

Such analysis is an important component in planning your career with a company. For one, it helps you understand how you can affect a company's growth. It helps you to (a) locate different parts of the company where your skills would be useful and (b) understand how broadly your skills are relevant to a company or even to an industry. It thus provides you with some understanding of how well your skills match with the company's profile and potential directions for your own growth. In an era where job cuts and layoffs have become usual, the importance of this cannot be overstated.

Consider the following exercise: Choose a company (or industry or organization within a company) of interest and explore all their products and services. (If you want to really get into this, you can even look up the sales numbers for these products; it will give you a value of the skills you consider.) Now list all problems or challenges associated with making and selling such a product. For a paint manufacturing company, these would include design of paint particles, formulation of paints and additives, stability of paints, and testing of properties of these paints. Now list your skills that are relevant to solving these problems, and there you have an understanding of the value you could bring to the paint industry.

You could use the format in Figure 3.1 to perform this analysis, and it would be worth sharing this with candidate

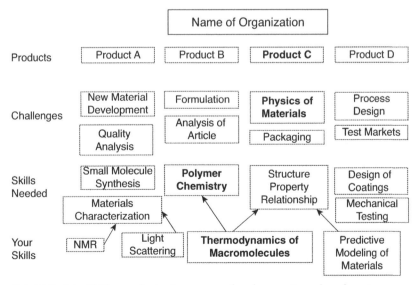

FIGURE 3.1. Skills analysis in career development and value to an organization.

companies to show them the value you could bring to them. (In this template, we have used more dominant fonts to articulate more important products or challenges faced by the company as well as skills that become more valuable to the company.) In the exercise described, we have focused primarily on technical challenges and skills. However, it is possible that patent strategy, market analysis, or commercialization experience are major needs and you have that experience. The template below can include those needs and skills as well for a more complete analysis.

This analysis helps you (a) identify critical skills that different industries need and (b) evaluate how valuable a person with your skills might be to these industries. You could now use this template to compare your value to a host of companies that may interest you. It can help define your strategy in choosing the right company for you and your growth plan. Can you identify industries or organizations that would most value your skills? Are your skills more valuable to organizations with a particular kind of business models?

Why is such an analysis necessary? We have realized that the industrial career is a complex career, sometimes nonlinear and often unpredictable and unknowable. In such a situation, while one can draw correlations that if one has certain skills, one will do well, one cannot predict that you will achieve a certain position in the corporate ladder with your skill set. Within this environment of unpredictability, every venture is risky and has a small chance of success. Through this exercise, then, you have developed a broader understanding of your role in a potential company and increased your probability of success.

For example, consider a company that has a small fuel cells program, which is the only place in the company that needs inorganic catalysis expertise. Unless you plan on gaining other skills, this position is tenuous as far as your career is concerned. As economic trends change and the company strategy changed, this program could get deemphasized and you might realize that no one in that company finds your inorganic catalysis skills valuable any more. This tool, thus, helps you understand that the probability and opportunities to have a successful career within this company are small given your current skills set. As a corollary (and we will discuss this as well), it provides leads about new skills that you would need to develop to make your skills portfolio more robust and improve your probability for success.

One increases one's overall chances of success by design of ventures (whether these be skill development, technology development, product development, or any other economic effort) such that they can lead to multiple possible wins. For example, if I was considering spending my time learning a new skill, I would ask how many different new career options it would open up for me. Similarly, if I was considering developing a new technology, I would consider all possible products and market opportunities that may result. Thus, in planning your career, you should consider skills, job options, and potential programs that can perhaps lead you to more possible wins; You should also consider adjacent skills that will complement your core skills.

For this discussion, we will include as core skills those areas in which you would be considered an expert as well as those areas that you understand well enough and have experience required to work independently. From an industrial perspective, this is an appropriate definition since your role is to understand an area well enough to help develop products or make decisions to drive profits—the skills you would draw upon to achieve this are your core skills. Having acknowledged these as your core skills, take a look at opportunities for adjacent skill development. Figure 3.2 exemplifies such an analysis.

In listing adjacent skill opportunities, consider what other skills would be extensions of your current core areas of

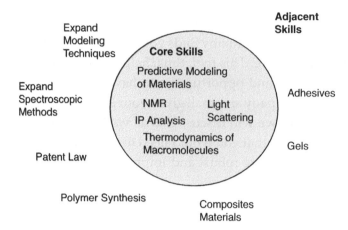

FIGURE 3.2. Opportunities for skills advancement based on analysis of core skills.

expertise. If you are an expert in Molecular Dynamics simulations, opportunities for skill development include Monte Carlo simulations, development of meso-scale models spanning multiple length scales and time domains, and so on. If you have experience in analyzing patents, you could expand your skills by either going into patent law (that gives you expertise to be a patent attorney) or perhaps focusing on patent strategy, and so on, as we populate our template as in Figure 3.3.

As we lay out these opportunities for skill development, we recognize that these opportunities have the potential to take us in different directions. Learning patent law and the potential of being a patent attorney would take us down a career path very different from the career paths that might open up with increased understanding of composite materials. The next step in using this tool is to analyze the potential career opportunities that these skills empower.

The opportunity analysis of skill development brings up some very interesting questions and pointers. Expanding modeling techniques leads to a number of diverse options: in predicting structure and performance of materials (core to

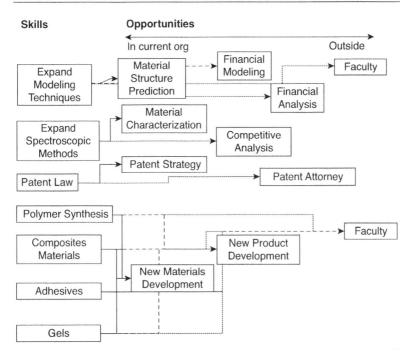

FIGURE 3.3. Career opportunities map based on choices in skill advancement.

product development), in a career in academia, in modeling of internal finances, in scenario mapping with new products, or in financial analysis of markets. In terms of breadth of opportunities, this skill advancement can potentially lead to a wide variety of opportunities, which is good for your portfolio. On the other hand, it is important for you to ask how interested you may be in these radically different jobs.

In addition, it is important to ask how a certain skill is valued in the company: Is it critical to its strategies or seen as "enabling" and nice to have? If staying and growing within the organization is important, then you should weigh areas that are core to the company or those that seem to be growing appropriately in making this decision. If there are major technology developments in a certain area, which you believe can be incorporated into current interests (products, technologies), this may be another reason to pursue a certain technology. You might also weigh this choice with external opportunities that may be available as you build on this. If you consider going outside the current organization, you want to consider how this skill is currently viewed outside, as well as what trends one observes in terms of areas relevant to this skill.

It is also critical to consider interdisciplinary opportunities that may arise by adding new skills with your core skills. In fact, this might be the biggest reason to follow a certain path. For example, there might be thousands of researchers working in composites, perhaps numerous in your own company. What you bring to the table depends on how you can leverage your understanding of thermodynamics of macromolecules and your modeling skills to develop new composites. Would there be career options in Figure 3.3 from interdisciplinary considerations of new skill complementing your core?

Finally, it is also important to ask how opportunities or openings in a company of choice may align with these skills. For example, consider Figure 2.4 or 2.6: Are there sections of the market in which a given company does not participate? Is there opportunity for growth in these gaps, and how can your skills support it? Or is the gap not aligned to company strategy or interest? Where would the company consider growing in the next few years, and how do your skills align with these interests?

The major filters in helping you understand the relevance of these choices for you include:

- Does this skill help you broaden your skill portfolio— within the organization *and* outside the organization?
- How valuable is this skill to your organization?
- What technology and market trends affect opportunities resulting from this skill?
- Do they overlap with your interests?

- Do the career opportunities align with your longer-term goals?

It is never too early to start analyzing your skills advancement options, and such a tool could help you analyze these options before deciding which one makes the most sense for your career and your life. A career is a dynamic and long-term process. A successful career requires that you consistently and for most part meet your lifetime needs. Yet, it is a dynamic process in that your focus and the activities that define your career are able to adapt to meet the demands of your career and your life needs.

In these times of fast-changing markets and corporations constantly adjusting to these, there is a continuous emphasis and deemphasis of programs implying volatility in employment. Lifetime employment has become less expected—and not as common. That implies that employees need to evaluate lifetime employability. It is thus imperative that you constantly evaluate what parallel livelihoods are possible, which ones are feasible (from your needs perspective and external trends), and what skills do you need to access them. Look at the next level and consider the skills and responsibilities needed at that level. Then make appropriate decisions on where you should be and on your skill development plan.

YOUR PERSONALITY AND YOUR CAREER CHOICES

It is useful to think about your personality with respect to the culture of companies of interest. Some coaches and authors have argued that your personality may not be right for certain jobs; often, real-life experience run counter to such a claim. You can choose any job, irrespective of your personality, as long as you are conscious of it and know how to work with that personality trait. Your personality does affect how you do your job, but understanding your personality and needs of your job can help you find appropriate paths to get the job done; in fact it may make you more effective.

A successful manager in a Fortune 100 company once described that early in his career, people had decided that he was a quiet but thoughtful person and was not aggressively assertive but when he had something to say, it was well thought out and of great value. His boss at that time was one with such an opinion. The boss stated that, given his personality, he would not be good at managing people but would be a very good scientist. In fact, this boss recommended that he not be given managerial opportunities.

His next boss had other opinions and pointed out to this man that being soft-spoken did not mean he could not manage, just as being outspoken or loud did not mean an individual could manage well. This man since has developed his own style of managing. He recognized that his primary roles as a manager included (a) developing new technologies that could be successfully commercialized and (b) helping develop people in his group; he also recognized that neither of these roles required him to be outspoken or an extrovert. His due diligence in understanding market opportunities and product needs, combined with true understanding of technologies, helped develop strong tech-nology pipelines. His strategic plans were often recognized as some of the best in that section of the company. He helped revitalize a core technology area in the company. His understanding of the opportu-nity, strategic planning, data, and analysis more than made up for his nonaggressive demeanor.

His "soft-spoken-ness" and humility allowed him to be inclusive of members of his team and truly learn from them. The members of his team did not feel that he was out to turn the focus of every discussion on to himself; this helped him build strong relationships with his team. In addition, his soft-spoken demeanor did not stop him from having hard conversations during conflicts between team members, nor did it prevent him from strongly advocating for his team. This earned him a reputation for being a manager who stood up for his team.

Personality does not define whether you can do or cannot do a certain job. It could influence strategies you choose to do it. For example, an introverted person could be a salesman. In recognizing that he is introverted, he may not be able to smooth-talk his way into a sale (as an extrovert might). He might require more data and analysis and may have to build a case based on that data. But perhaps that could turn out to be his strength and lead to success in ways that an extrovert could never imagine. He might even need to adapt by practicing making presentations, designing digressions or jocular moments into his talk. He might need to spend more time truly understanding market segments and customers needs. But this understanding can help design new products or offerings.

The problem is that often we are not conscious of our personality traits and how they affect our job, and hence we are not conscious of the role of our personality traits or of optimal strategies that are consistent. Instead, we attempt to use a leadership style described in a rule book or in some leadership course. In this context, it may be useful for you to study a variety of coaches in your favorite sport. You will find men and women with very different personalities—some who are publicly reserved, others who yell and shout, some who quietly sit during a game, others who keep pacing nervously or aggressively. You will find that all of these types can be successful: Their differing personalities seem not to have hindered their progress because they are conscious of their personalities and provide leadership styles that are consistent.

If you are looking at a specific job or you have started on this job, it might be useful for you to go through the exercise described in Table 3.1. Use the first column to list your

TABLE 3.1. EXAMPLE OF HOW STRATEGIES CAN BE USED TO TRANSCEND
PERSONALITY TRAITS

Perceived Personality/ Traits	Job Requirements	Strategies
Reserved	Project planning	Develop discipline, understand scope of project, define milestones and deadlines
Does not have the ability to "drive" people	Project management	Gather collective expertise, drive decision making
Soft-spoken	Motivating team	Data-driven decision making, share reasons for decisions, transparent decision making, delegate leadership for various subprojects
Does not feel too connected with people	Conflict resolution	Use win–win style techniques for conflict resolution; be sensitive to people's needs
Not an articulate/ effective oral communicator	Presentation of team results	Complement verbal with written, use figures and data
Is not a good "leader"	Understanding, articulation of team plans	Use scenario mapping, extensive data-driven conclusions

personality traits. Use the second column to list the requirements or nature of the job. Use the third column, then, to briefly
describe how your personality can help you do the job or how
you can adapt to do the job. Table 3.1 shows such an analysis for
a team leader of a technology development team.

One final comment: It is necessary to differentiate between your personality and your attitude. Being grumpy or rude or a gossip is not a personality—it is an attitude or a habit. Attitude should not be an excuse for failure.

YOUR VALUES AND YOUR CAREER

There is much to be said about values in your career. Of course, companies talk about ethics and they often have mandatory courses on ethics and values. However, these are often to ensure compliance with government regulations—a result of increasingly strict laws on sexual harassment, discrimination of various kinds and of late, and laws on ethical accounting. Whether a company is truly ethical is a question that perhaps cannot be answered. Often companies participate in ways where they play within the laws, but push for increasing profits and lobby to change laws. One often sees that companies will follow policies in the countries of the global south which would be completely unacceptable in North America or Europe. For example, large Fortune 100 companies are known to sell products in South Asia and in sub-Saharan Africa which are banned in North America or Europe for reasons of health hazards. It is not as if employees themselves are unethical. However, within the framework of profit making and Wall Street carrots, the pressure to sell is huge and if it is legal, it is deemed ethical.

Well-known management guru Peter Drucker says that values defined his own career.[24] He left an investment banking job during the 1930's depression to do something he truly valued. Values are not ethics—ethics should be the same for all. Values are the core principles that you believe are important to you. Ethics in one organization and for one individ-

---

[24] P. F. Drucker, *Management Challenges for the 21st Century*, Harper Collins, 1999.

ual should be the same in another organization or another individual. Ethics form only part of the value system. Drucker says that "To work in an organization whose value system is unacceptable or incompatible with one's own condemns a person both to frustration and to nonperformance." Yet, one may be very successful at what one does and still find that this does not fit in with one's value system. One might find jobs where one does well but where one finds no way to connect with one's values. For example, one might truly care about development of kids but be working in the fabrication facility of a semiconductor industry and be very successful in one's career. To the extent that this gives rise to frustration, one should consciously attempt to find a job that relates to ones values.

There may be even more extreme cases where the goals of the organization or one's job is counter to one's values. This could lead to significant frustration and even though one could keep on plugging away, persistent frustration will lead to nonperformance. Drucker says that values should be the ultimate test in deciding one's career path and that one's success will be affected by this decision.

A senior former employee of a Fortune 100 company described the importance of values in conversations with us. When he retired, he had fulfilled director level roles for that company in various global positions. He had also served on the city council and had run for the mayor of the city where he lived. He had clear self-professed convictions about serving the community and described himself as highly environmentally conscious.

During his career, he had a number of opportunities where speeding up development of products or processes would have meant quicker profits for the company. However, in many of these cases, this would have been at the cost of environmental concerns. Sometimes, products were developed based on raw materials that might have a significant impact on the environment during the life cycle of the product. At other times, consumers would not be affected but the process of manufacturing might impact the environment. In each case he chose to take the safer path. The safer path often meant significant new R&D to change the raw material or make the process safer. The company also supported that path; however, this former employee felt that the company's support was driven more by the realization that shortcuts might cost the company significantly in suits and in reputation.

During this discussion, though, he made a point that is worth recognizing. The pressure to succeed—often self- imposed pressure—is very high. Often, in the context of this self-imposed pressure, individuals are willing to sacrifice their values. This is not just on environmental issues—it includes ethical behavior that transcends ideologies, such as accounting, documentation, and environmental issues, as well as whether we give credit to our colleagues.

STRATEGY MAPS

We started this chapter by asking, Who are you? In a career setting, this question is only meaningful to the extent that it helps you understand the question, Where do you want to be? How will you be what you want to be? How do you get to be in that state and how do you maintain that state? Strategy maps are useful in helping us envision how we can be where we want to be. Whether the goal is short term ("I want to get product A commercialized") or longer term ("I want to be a lead scientists or a group leader"), strategy maps lay out scenarios and help you assess different paths that can help these goals.

Look at the example of a career strategy map (Figure 3.4), drawn out by our candidate. This shows her current situation (skills, strengths) and accessible opportunities at the very bottom of the map and her life needs at the very top. Based on these life needs, we see that this individual wants to be a group leader developing new technologies in a large corporate

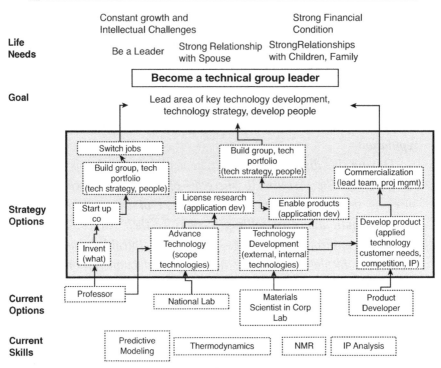

FIGURE 3.4. Example of a career strategy map.

R&D lab. The figure also shows that the specific goal is considered in the context of her life needs.

As our wannabe group leader strategizes on getting to her goals, she can only begin with the skills she has and the job options that are possible for such set of skills. The gray box is then the strategy box—options that are available to her and how they get her to her goal of being a group leader. Each position or responsibility requires learning of specific skills; the map shows pathways that allow for learning of these skills. This being a high-level view, there is much detailed planning to be done regarding various options; for example, if she founded a start-up, what would be the activities of the start-up, in what markets do they play, and how do they impact her ability to become a group leader in a large corporate lab? If she became a researcher in a national lab, what area of technology should she scope and advance in a way that is industrially relevant? Similarly, if she started off as a materials scientist or a product developer, she would have some options to grow—she must choose what kinds of technologies or products she should develop, what would be aligned with her current organization, how she might want to move between organizations, where she might find opportunities to commercialize the product she developed, and so on. Based on her broader knowledge of careers, which of these pathways would have a higher probability of success?

Having recognized these strategies that she can access, our protagonist can then assess which jumps between positions are most feasible (How easy is it to move from a national lab to be a group leader in the corporate world? How many people have done this?), which ones provide her with numerous pathways to achieving her goal, and so on. Her decision would then be based on this analysis.

The framework in setting up a career strategy map is valuable in prioritizing options, setting up skill advancement opportunities, building networks, and making choices. The features of this strategy are not salient to becoming a group leader—they are true for all such goals. Hence, maintaining a diversity of skills at your level of leadership becomes necessary to consider alternatives and increase your probability of success. Within a chaotic system which is exemplified by industrial careers, this becomes especially true.

MODEL CAREERS

There is no predictive modeling of careers—we have already established that. Perhaps the closest attempt would be to gain heuristic knowledge based on other careers. Getting to know profiles of numerous individuals will help you build a working career strategy. It is therefore quite instructive to study the career trajectories of people at different stages of their careers within a company who began with similar skill sets as you do. Often, such a study of diverse career paths will help you recognize which of the multiple paths explored in your career strategy map have high probability of success. Figure 3.5 shows an example of a career profile. Make sure that as you study a set of career profiles, include in your set people who have had different levels of "success" in their careers.

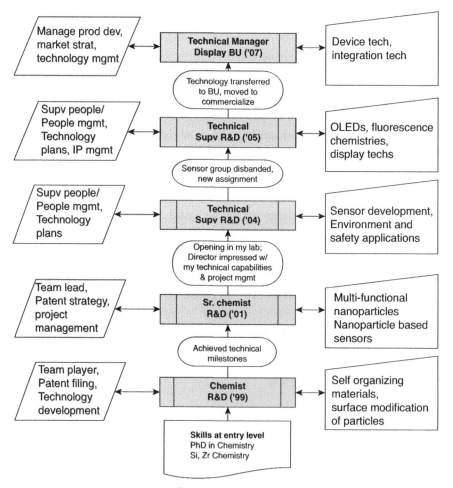

FIGURE 3.5. Example of a career profile.

This analysis is based on understanding what technical and business skills were learned at each stage as people moved to the next.[25] As you study the profiles of a few careers, look at the variety of opportunities that are accessed by this group at different levels—that is, how many diverse paths were taken by people who started with similar skills and a similar position? In addition, notice if there was a particular point in the careers where most paths diverged. For example, it is quite possible that the first two levels of jobs were quite similar for most people (in terms of responsibilities and kind of skills learned). This analysis is important by itself: It lets you review your plan and assess which career strategies are most viable. In addition, it asks whether there are strategies accessible within this company that you had not included within your plan and gives you an opportunity to review them vis-à-vis your own needs.

Consider, also, career paths of people you perceive as intelligent who have not done so well in moving up the corporate ladder. Where did their growth slow down and why? Did they make choices that allowed for a more suitable work–life equilibrium for themselves? Did they work on certain kinds of projects? Did they have a certain work-style or a certain way of doing things? How did they interact with other peers and with their management? This will provide significant information about what may impede growth in your career as well as tell you about the culture of the company: What kinds of activities and behavior do they encourage or discourage? How do they react to honest critique, for example?

Figure 3.5 describes the skills of the individual in starting his career, the position of the individual, and the organization into which his career moved with the time line. At each position, it describes the technical and other skills learned on the job and

[25]Most people will be happy to share this information with you as they talk to you about their careers.

the key achievements or scenarios that influenced his move to the next level.

In addition, if you know some of the people (whose career plans you review), you might also want to find out:

1. Were there gaps in their skills when they went to the next level? If so, what were these gaps? This could help you understand what other skills you should include in your own plans. In addition, it will also help you assess whether the nature of those jobs have changed in your company since this individual's experience and account for them in your plan.

2. What were the conditions that aided or inhibited or otherwise affected this move? Often, moves in the early portion of one's career are quite "automatic," where people get their first couple promotions fairly quickly and with ease. However, as one continues to grow, factors other than performance also become important—reflecting the fact that there are fewer jobs and less opportunity to move higher as one moves up the ladder. These include the business environment at that time and the state of the economy as well as access to the opportunities that do open up (how well hiring managers know you). Thus, it is important to ask how such experiences influenced the growth opportunities in this individual's profile. In addition, it is quite possible that the individual took advantage of trends internally or externally within the company. For example, we have discussed how individuals in companies took advantage of certain programs being instituted to aid their career growth. Alternatively, people have also used external trends (such as a sudden need for greater security or changes in health-care policies) to institute programs

that have led to their growth. Or sometimes, individuals were just lucky: They were at the right place at the right time and the move surprised them.

Often people will be willing to talk to you about their careers in organizations. You do not have to ask pointed questions; genuine interest in how they grew and how they sought opportunities is enough. As you gain this information, relate it with your own situation. This will also help you add strategic components to your plan.

A word of caution though: These case studies of careers of others can only provide heuristic data. So while they can help you build in strategy options into your plans, be wary of focusing on a strategy that will get you there based on a few case studies. Or be wary of building your expectations based on these profiles. As you look through these profiles, you will notice that the needs and trends of career growth change as you look at people in different stages of their careers. In different times during a company's life, its needs and its demographics change. For those who joined a company in its early days, perhaps growth was faster because there were fewer people. Or perhaps, there was a certain time when the demographics of the company changed and a lot of people retired. Or there were major layoffs a few years before, and those who were left grew when the company started growing and hiring again.

Also beware that when you study the profiles of executives, you will find that they will have grown super-rapidly. In large companies, an individual will need perhaps 10 promotions in 20 or 30 years to get to the position of an executive by the time she in her fifties. That is not common; it often means that such people had a strong network and that a variety of reasons helped them grow in this fashion. Use these profiles to understand what paths had higher probability of such growth—

remembering that with changing times, the success through those paths may have changed. Also, use these profiles to learn what may have helped them grow and thus strategize accordingly—but remember that there is no guarantee that if you do the same, you will grow in the same way.

SUMMARY

How fulfilling your career will be depends largely on how well you understand your skills and your needs. This chapter largely focuses on providing tools and a framework of analysis to help you understand your needs and your strengths and weaknesses and then trying to understand how jobs may or may not align with those needs and those skills. It does not prescribe which decision is right or wrong for you or what job is appropriate for you. There is no formula that can predict that. However, going through the tools described can help you identify for yourself what kinds of careers would be meaningful for your needs and your dreams.

In addition, we also explored skills and development strategies you could use to achieve your career goals, given your current skill sets. This helps set up your career strategy map, all the while recognizing that these goals are dynamic and what options and opportunities present themselves depend on a number of things outside your control. However, as a knowledge worker, you have the privilege to find and define a career that is fulfilling if it is built based on your needs and your strengths and weaknesses.

KEY TAKEAWAYS

1. What would you do if you did not have to earn money? What are your major life dreams? They provide clues to

what a fulfilling career and life would mean for you. Use this understanding to shape your career as well as to plan your life and understand the role of your career in your life.

2. Recognize that the goals of your career and how you achieve them have to be consistent with your life needs and dreams. While there will be variations, recognize those variations and why you make choices that lead to those variations. Otherwise, you will face internal conflicts and frustration. A successful career for you cannot be defined by money, fame, power, or any such parameter. It is one that is consistent with your life equilibrium *at any time.*

3. Understand your skills and how they relate to the key goal of a company—to make profits. What kinds of activities are part of the company's strategy in making profits? What problems of a company do your skills help you solve? What broad classes of expertise can you bring to bear that will help a company? What broad segments of their markets do your skills impact? This helps you truly understand how you can be a part of a company's plans; it also helps you articulate your potential roles in a company more concisely and in a language that is of interest to the industry.

4. Your resume is a document articulating these skills for a specific market. What markets or organizations would be interested in your resume? How would you rewrite your resume based on this discussion?

5. What are you core skills? What careers options are available to you based on your core skills? Which of these options are consistent with your life needs and your dreams? What adjacent skills are of interest? Who values these skills—within an organization and

outside? What career options are feasible based on these adjacent skills?

6. In analyzing your skills with respect to a company's needs, you also begin to understand what potential for growth you have in a company. What variety and classes of problems can you solve? How much does the company truly need your skills? If you choose to be in a company, what potential paths of growth are available and what skill development is necessary for you to access those paths? It helps you in career planning.

7. Your personality does not limit your career options. It cannot be a reason or an excuse to do or not do certain jobs. However, it can influence the strategy you choose in a specific job to deliver the goals expected from that job. Consider your personality and recognize what strategies you can use to achieve deliverables within the comfort of your personality.

8. Values are the core principles by which you live your life—what is most important to you and what will guide your life choices. Choose a career that is consistent with your values; it will lead to least internal conflict and frustration and potentially more satisfaction.

9. Connect your skills with the problem needs of a company to build a career strategy map. Consider adjacent skill development opportunities to broader potential paths to achieve your goals. Consider skills needs at various levels to ask what development plan you should undertake. Use your values as a guide to recognize which paths are more satisfying and consistent with who you are. Allow a dynamic strategy map for you career to guide your short- and medium-term development plan.

10. Consider model careers of peers and senior colleagues in your company with similar skill sets to study feasibility of various paths in your strategy map. What career options are available to people with such skills? What were important skills needed to perform at a certain level and how did they acquire those skills? Were there skills that usually opened up certain career paths? Were there specific conditions at a certain time that catalyzed or inhibited career paths? How have expectations from these positions changed over time? Allow these considerations to further define your strategy map.

STARTING OUT

As you start your new job, you either feel excited about the possibilities or you feel bittersweet since you had hoped for something better or different. If it is the former, you will be excited about starting your job. If it is the latter, be conscious of that negative feeling and recognize that it could translate into inaction and an unwillingness to be proactive; that would make it even more difficult for you to move to that dream job. Even if this is not the job you would wish for, use this opportunity to learn the skills you need to get to your next job. And show that you can solve problems. Industrial leaders want problem solvers who will act, not people who are given to sulking. Proven ability to solve problems in industrial settings will get you where you want to be.

We were told about a bright young chemical engineer who joined a small biochemistry firm. This was not a path-breaking start-up. Rather, it was an ultra-small company that provided gels to other start-ups and medium and large bio-companies to test their samples that enabled others to do their exciting work. It could hardly be the job that young engineers dream about. It seemed like one job that required as little chemical engineering as possible. You got customized orders,

Planning a Scientific Career in Industry: Strategies for Graduates and Academics
By Sanat Mohanty and Ranjana Ghosh
Copyright © 2010 John Wiley & Sons, Inc.

prepared the gels in batches based on the orders, and pack-
aged and shipped them. Yet this engineer committed himself
to understand what was expected of him, the context of his
work, the markets served, and key needs of this market. Over
time, he developed continuous processing to develop such
gels, thus improving turnaround times and higher
reproducibility of the gels. This led to more reliability, new
customers, and greater market penetration. The bright young
engineer was not frustrated that this was a dead-end job or
that he was not doing something more exciting. He addressed
an unarticulated problem by truly understanding the markets
and its product needs. And he met them by bringing in an
understanding that was outside the traditional fields that
usually engaged themselves with this market—and played
to his own strengths.

Irrespective of how you feel toward the job, unless you
show you can win, future opportunities will be much fewer.
After all, future employers would like to find someone who can
consistently take on problems and win, not someone who is
often not interested or whimsical. And unless you bring your A
self to the game, there is little chance that you can win consistently and thus establish yourself.

THE COMPANY AND A NEW EMPLOYEE

Starting in a new company is a new experience. Each organization will have its own landscape and its own culture; even if
you were joining with industrial experience in another company, you would have to learn this new landscape. A new
employee program is critical: It helps you understand this
new landscape.

As a new employee, it would be pertinent to find out
whether the company has such a program. Almost every company will have one. In many companies though, it will usually

be a half-day or one-day program run by the Human Resources department and will be scheduled during your first few days on the job. This will cover some general aspects such as benefits, legal aspects of information sharing, discrimination, company codes, and policies. It rarely addresses career issues that you need to know as a new employee, because its main goal is to check off boxes that inform new employees about its policies. It provides no strategic learning for your career development.

Some other companies might have a plan that (a) introduces you to people in a group and their jobs and (b) exposes you to logistical and administrative tools that are relevant to your job. This is better than nothing, but it is not truly focused on your growth—it is focused on training you just enough so that you can begin to do the job you need to do. For new employees in companies that do not have robust orientation programs, this section provides knowledge about your job that you should seek out to accelerate your own development.

A senior scientist at a Fortune 100 company told of his experience the first year he joined this company, after having worked in a different industry for a few years:

> On my first day, I met contact persons from different departments— HR, finance, and administrative. They told me all about my benefits, how I should be recording time in timesheets, where the cafeteria was, and what days the bagel club met. That was all good, but what struck me as strange was that I was never really formally introduced to my group members. I was assigned to a project, with most of the team members being from a different office location. I was starting to get to know people, when the project suddenly ran short of funds and was abruptly stopped.
>
> The initial few months after that incident were very challenging in terms of hunting for projects, writing proposals for funds from external agencies, and at the same time worrying about "being on the bench" for too long. Not knowing the culture of the organization, as well as not

knowing people or groups, added to the stress, as did the time it took to finally start working on a project in line with my skills and interest. Not having a support network made it difficult to succeed. The interim projects I worked on were ad hoc and required a different set of skills than what I had or was interested in.

A proper orientation would have helped prepare me for this challenge in my first year, and knowledge of the group's working culture would have helped me make decisions different from those I made and thus saved me precious months of agony in my first year here. Not knowing the culture certainly affected my initial career path and took a longer than ideal amount of time to rectify.

A good orientation program needs to help you be successful immediately while also helping longer-term growth by providing you multiple paths to achieve your potential. The short-term component of the program provides the employee with a framework to function and to ably perform the first set of responsibilities. The immediate aspects would include standard tools and procedures. It should introduce you to various people in the immediate group—to stakeholders, collaborators, and decision makers in all your programs. It should also introduce you to all resources that you do not have to use but can have access to—including databases and lists, archives of different kinds, and so on. It should also introduce you to the culture of the immediate group including:

1. What the group does and how its success is measured.
2. How is your performance measured, by what process, and who has input in the process?
3. The context in which the group operates; for example, if this group provides IT support to an engineering function, it is important to understand the general activities of the engineering function, its plans forward, relationship between the groups, nature of requests, and so on.

4. How the group does its job: What are its strategies? how is it organized to succeed? How has it built alliances and with whom? How does it share information? How are its programs run? and so on.

5. Who are individuals whose opinions are important for this group?

The longer-term component should provide an understanding of what makes employees successful in your company (metrics and programs that help understand your role in the profit-making path of the company), potential career options, tools you could use in the next few years to grow, and those that help build your network in the company. The orientation program should span a year to give you time to learn about experiences that do not all happen in the first month of your start. It should have at least the following components:

1. Gives you (a) information about the structure of the company, your specific group, and your role as well as the roles of other organizations, (b) a description of how you interact with the rest of the company and the world, and (c) information regarding how all of this is part of the plan to make profits. In essence, it is describing your role in the profit-making universe.

2. Provides a support base (through other new employees and veterans) to help you understand how your industrial role is different from your academic experience and what skills you would need to learn to help you become successful. This could include classes on team work, discussions on leadership, presentations on how to manage your time in the face of multiple responsibilities, classes on proposal writing, and so on. This perhaps is the most important piece of new employee training.

3. Helps you build a network of people who complement what you do best and whose work you can support and strategically help. In addition, also helps you build a network with people who can help you grow.

4. Helps you understand career options in the company and identify and map skills that would help you pursue those career options.

5. Help you learn the unwritten rules that define how people interact and how the company is run in real time and through honest interactions.

Numerous IT companies actually spend between 1 and 6 months at the start of a new employee's career training the employee. During this time, the employee may be on "probation" and may be paid only half to three-quarters of her salary. Training includes technical aspects of the function. In addition, they also include other aspects of being successful with and for the organization. Given that many large IT companies have global clients, they provide extensive training on global culture—from how to eat and what to wear to how to interact and about values and traditions. Numerous IT companies also include social and networking aspects within their training modules. Thus, there is focus on developing "soft" skills related to conversations, connecting with colleagues and with clients, building relationships, developing networks, and accessing those networks for business opportunities for the company as well as for personal growth.

This time of training is invaluable for new employees. Since these companies hire a significant number of new employees from different cultures, the focused training sessions provide an opportunity to help them integrate into the corporate culture as well as learn the culture of global organizations. In addition, it helps these individuals build their first network—among their own peers. Through joint problem solving and learning, they teach each other and grow, laying the groundwork for collaboration later on. Through this network, they learn how to deal with new clients, new cities, and new cultures. The network provides a home to many of these employees; and in an industry with high turnover, it is seen to provide some sense of belonging and loyalty. Most of all, it helps the new employees learn the culture of the organization.

PERFORMANCE METRICS

Proactively planning your career requires that you be cognizant of the metrics used to measure an individual in a company. Almost all companies have performance metrics. While they will vary significantly, there are two aspects we should understand: What does it measure and who all provide input?

In most large companies, performance metrics have two broad components:

1. Specific level of contribution for the year that measures performance in your projects:
   (a) Did you meet or exceed expectations?
   (b) How did you perform against your goals?
   (c) Were you a primary contributor to progress, and did you support a program or enable it?
   (d) Did you have major breakthroughs during the year, and so on.

2. More general measurement of your skills that include:
   (a) Your technical capabilities and knowledge and how you apply these to invent, innovate, solve problems.
   (b) How you understand the market and customer needs, scope problems, and attempt to solve them.
   (c) How you take initiative and are able to lead peers, people who do not report to you, people who are senior to you, and so on.

(d) How people respond to you, whether you put them off, how you collaborate with people, communication skills.

(e) How you uphold and follow the culture of the organization, your "community" involvement in the company (are you involved with diversity groups, environment initiatives, and other programs not directly related to your role and not among your stated goals?).

Different organizations may bundle these differently, may weight these differently, or may have variations on these metrics. In general, however, the HR community sees these as robust indicators of performance that can provide feedback to the employee and to the company about the performance and the potential of an employee. For a new employee, that is key motivation to understanding the performance metrics in your company and how the metrics are evaluated. The rest of this chapter and the next will essentially provide insight into skills and tools that can help you manage your performance with respect to these metrics as well as build your career.

In managing your performance, it is also important to know who evaluates you. In some companies, it is only your group leader or manager. In others, some significant component is based on peer evaluation. In yet others, it could also include input from the projects in which you work and your internal and external customers. It is important to understand this component of performance management and hence appropriately manage expectations and delivery with those stakeholders. After all, it is not just how you believe you have performed. It is also important to appropriately represent your performance to those stakeholders.

You, The Problem Solver

As a new employee, your first task is to (a) confirm to the people who hired you that you are the right person to do the job and (b) confirm to your peers and the company leadership that you are the right person who can solve a wide variety of critical problems optimally. In the context of discussions in earlier sections, your ticket to a great career is to be recognized as a problem solver who can help the organization grow. Your peers, people you lead as well as key decision makers, must recognize that you can solve critical and difficult problems and trust your solution. This implies that you are able to do the following:

1. *Recognize problems and scope and define them accurately, not just attempting to solve an apparent or articulated problem.* Often the apparent problem is only a perception (even a simplification) of the real problem by someone who is not an expert. As with all other parts of life, this non-expert will observe only part of the problem, interpret what it could mean, and then state that interpretation with some component of the observation as the problem. A discussion with any experienced scientist or engineer will throw up numerous such examples. An attempt to address the problem as articulated will often result in failure, simply because it does not identify issues at the core.

It is also important to understand the scope of the solution by understanding the context of the problem. For example, a certain product may have some flaws. The solution might require a complete redesign, but is that feasible? If a redesigned product needs 12 months for development, can the market wait that long? What will be the impact of this wait? Is a quick-fix solution—while neither ideal nor addressing all the flaws—possible? In an ideal world, perhaps both should be undertaken; but in reality, one has to look at which solution can one truly influence. If one is in an organizational setting that only allows for short-term quick fix, then perhaps one needs to leverage support so that another group addresses the redesign. The scope of the solution is thus dependent on the context of the problem and the practical aspect of the solution. Choosing the inappropriate scope leads to ineffective solutions.

2. *Look at the problem holistically, and evaluate a variety of solutions to address the problem.* Unless you see the holistic picture (all aspects of the product and its supply chain), your solution might resolve some immediate issues but cause damage to other parts of the system. On the other hand, using a holistic systems approach, you might need to leverage appropriate outside expertise to guide the solution. Sometimes, suggestions from outside bring in new perspectives to the problem resulting in breakthrough innovations. You understand the impact of these possible solutions and choose the solution with strategic consideration.

3. *Recognize the impact of the problem, and prioritize* it with respect to other problems. It is important that you can understand the importance and enormity of the problem in the context of the big picture and react commensurately. If the problem could cause even temporary shutdown of a line or a plant, often hundreds of thousands to millions of dollars are at risk. On the other hand, if a batch of faulty products has been sent to a customer, while the risk is still significant, it is more manageable. Or if a key person in the lab has had sudden reasons to miss a few days, while it affects work, it is not usually a crisis.

It is equally important to recognize that one may not fully know the impact of more complex problems and one may have to use more complex strategies (discussed in Chapter 2) to engage with these problems. For example, how will a

certain activity affect a market and help your own organization grow (will it cannibalize your own products or affect
your competition in a specific way)? It may require some
initial engagement and future efforts based on initial feedback. Or it may require key collaborations. In any case, it
requires effective leadership.

4. *Implement the solution.* You have the wherewithal to
address technical hurdles as they arise and deliver the
solution. As difficult as it is to invent, developing a commercially viable product is also quite challenging and
requires immense engineering to meet rigorous industry
standards and demands. Often, this also requires you to go
beyond the charter of your "position," directly helping
with scale-up or organizing prototype studies, to ensure
success. You should be able to keep the team motivated
and driven to achieve this. In addition, you should be able
to implement the solution by acquiring buy-in from all
stakeholders, even when your solution may not seem like
the best one or may be in conflict with needs of some
stakeholders. For example, it could displace the current
technology, and those who own and drive the current
technology might be an influential group opposing your
solution.

The criteria to ensure that you have established yourself in
the industry are vastly different from those at school. You will
recognize that being a problem solver requires multiple intelligences: technical, emotional, social, and so on. In school,
your credibility depended on your ability to technically or
theoretically implement a solution to a problem. You did not
have to worry about difficult team dynamics, nor did you have
to address buy-in from key stakeholders to operationalize
your solution. Even in defining your problem and evaluating

solutions, you were often biased by interests of your group
and methods that were core to your group. You worried very
little on a day-to-day basis about what other groups might
be doing. The industry requires you to learn other skills to
be successful in establishing yourself.

KNOW YOUR GROUP

Numerous Human Resource reports suggest that the biggest
reason employees leave any job is owing to their immediate
supervisor. The group dynamics within which the job is situated can also positively or negatively influence this decision.
Thus, as a new employee, it is important that one understand
the role of the manager and the dynamics of the group where
the job will be situated.

KNOW YOUR MANAGER

It is important to understand the personality of your immediate
supervisor, how she sees her role as a manager, and what kind
of management approach she takes. Some managers lean
towards micromanaging every aspect of their group's efforts.
Some take a completely hands-off approach, letting members of
their group figure it out. And yet some others are able to take a
dynamic approach—getting involved in details when the
group needs that help and dynamically being hands-off depending on how the group is doing. Your supervisor's management style thus affects both the nature of support you
get and the efficacy of your working style.

It is important to understand what your manager thinks
his role should be. Does he give you frank feedback? When
you are doing well, does he tell you exactly what you are doing
well? Does he also point out specific areas where you could
improve or where you are just not making it? Will he have

difficult conversations about your performance throughout the course of the year? Or will he surprise you with a bad annual appraisal? How do you find out how your manager functions? Ask him about his style of management and how he starts difficult or frank discussions. And ask him how you did in your interview or in your first week at work; it will give you some pointers.

It is a good idea to try and understand where your manager may be in her career track. If she is pushing to aggressively grow in the company, she may be much more demanding of you. At the same time, she *may* also be willing to advocate for you. On the other hand, your manager might have come to a point in their career where she would like to "equilibrate." She may not want to take on more responsibilities (possibly for personal or other reasons) or may have come to realize that it is unlikely that she will advance further. In either case, she might have a more laid back style of management and probably be less demanding of you. At this stage in their career, such managers may be good mentors to you and/ or they might be less sensitive to your desire of aggressive growth. In any case, the place your manager may be in her career may affect your career. There are no easy ways to learn this information besides just getting to know your manager. It is, however, important to understand this because it can help you work with your manager to meet your goals.

KNOW YOUR TEAM

Your team plays a very influential role in your day-to-day work and hence your success. Recognize at the outset that you may be part of multiple teams playing different roles. Perhaps in one team you are part of the core mission, your role being critical to the team. In such situations, it is important to understand the role of each member, his or her contribution to the team, and his or her relationship with other members. In other situations, perhaps you provide a support or enabling role to the team as an outside expert or consultant. In such cases you may choose not to invest too much time in knowing such teams and their members. Recognize, however, that in a dynamically changing world where jobs and projects continue to be emphasized and deemphasized, knowing the teams and their members more than casually might help with your next job.

You should understand how a team contributes to the profit motive of the company and how it is aligned to the company's strategies. Identify whether the group's mission and activities are aligned to production or maintenance, growth of the company or in a support and enabling role for the company. The goals of the group and the work pressure often define the character of the group. For example, if the group is involved in manufacturing with tight schedules and timelines, with little time for exploratory work, innovation will happen on the fly and solutions will be developed as things happen. Or if the group is involved in technical support, there may not be the same pressure as in a manufacturing group but there will be pressures related to customer needs and specifications and changes in those, if any. Based on this understanding, identify how your role in the team is aligned with the company's strategy and contributes to its profits.

While the nature of jobs in different teams differs depending on their strategic alignment with the company's goal, the energy, the can-do attitude, the cynicism, and the burnout can be characteristics of all of these groups. It is important, then, to find out how the group characterizes itself and how other groups characterize it. A good place to start is to find out what the group's last three successes might have been—and how long ago they were. Ascertain in your own mind what the magnitude of these successes may have been. If the group is associated with growth, find out what major products the group may have commercialized in the past. Was the whole group involved or only a key few? If it is an R&D group, what does it develop technology for (commercialization or merely patents) and with whom does it collaborate? What might be key technical challenges that the group is attempting to address or what were some key challenges in the past that the group addressed? Is there enthusiasm about current problems the group works on, and do they see the importance of the problem for the technical challenges it brings or its impact on the company or both? These may help you understand the environment in which you will participate. It is also important to balance the self-image that the team may have with what other teams think about that team.

As with your manager, you should recognize the career trajectory and current coordinates of the people in your team. Are many of them at the end of their careers and spending their years waiting to retire? Or are they nearing the end of a successful career, trying to teach younger colleagues everything they know? Or are they ambitious colleagues on their way to success, willing to trample on everyone else to ensure they get all the limelight? Or are they ambitious in their career plans, and do they understand that their success can be more effective if their network or their team also grows? Or some combination of all these permutations and more that affects team dynamics? In exploring the successes of the team, find out about how it is measured and how the team manages to be successful. Are there conscious choices, deliberate strategies, and/or disciplined execution by the entire team that result in such successes? Or it is a result of the motivation, drive, or personality of one or two members that makes the team successful? Or is it just chance? Can the team articulate what makes it successful and talk about challenges or failures that have been learning opportunities. Can it mentor new employees to be successful?

A successful team has high energy and enthusiasm. It is focused on the problems and in exploring ways to address the problems. In being focused, it is able to quickly resolve and get around personnel issues. One of the biggest reasons that technical efforts fail is owing to team dynamics. In a successful team, members are willing to address or ignore differences between themselves in ways that keep the focus of the team on the problems and their solutions. A successful team has a healthy amount of cynicism that allows it to keep its problems and the implications of its success in perspective.

MANAGING EXPECTATIONS

We introduced you to new employee programs and the scenarios facing new employees. How do you manage these scenarios? This includes you actively seeking out your team leader, supervisor, or manager and beginning to understand and manage expectations from you. These include:

1. *Understanding your job and responsibilities* (both articulated and unarticulated ones because the latter are often more important than the former). Do you have a well-defined goal or do you have to define it or is it a mixture of the two? If it is well-defined, do you have any flexibility in further defining it? If you need to define it, then who provides input and how do you know that it is the right goal? Spend significant time with your manager or lead defining your expectations. Understand your role in the project and in the organization. Identify key stakeholders and leaders in your program. Visit with them and understand how they see the projects that are relevant to you and what they see as your role. Touch back with your supervisor on this.

This helps you ensure that all parties have the same expectations from this role as well as a clear understanding of what success looks like. In the absence of such a clear understanding, there will be conflicts about your goal and whether you have been successful, leading to much heartburn and potential failure. It is your job to manage this aspect of your role. Being new in a company means that you are getting to know people around you. You are also beginning to learn how to work in such an environment. Ensuring that there are clear measurements of short-term goals allows you to get better understanding about how people work, their priorities, and their expectations, as well as receive feedback about what you are doing and how your are doing it. Early feedback provides an opportunity for you to make progress and accomplish course correction. In the absence of that, you chance failure owing to reasons beyond your competence.

2. *Understanding the context of your job and responsibilities* (the context often defines the unarticulated responsibilities). It is important to understand what might be the motivations for these responsibilities or your projects. Often, if the goals are defined narrowly, you might achieve them and yet not be successful because the context within which the responsibilities were articulated may have changed or the larger goals may not have been met. It may thus be necessary for you to understand these broader goals and to work beyond your narrowly defined responsibilities to achieve success for yourself. If the motivation or the context is unclear, the project may change direction or scope significantly, thus affecting your ability to contribute. It may be necessary to understand who the primary stakeholders might be, how they are motivated about the project, and how they may be responsible for or influence the direction of the program.

For example, as part of the quality group for a launch team, you may have successfully implemented the test criteria by which the next great product will be measured. In that regard, you have been successful. However, if the product itself is not commercialized, you achievements will be in vain. Your development of test criteria is of no value when a product has not been launched.

When I first started my job, I was part of a group that was trying to develop a portfolio of products for my company to get into a new market segment. Along with another new employee, I was asked to work on development of new technologies to meet a well-defined need in a market segment that could potentially grow into a $20 million or more business. Over a period of 6 months, we had a few inventions and developed new technologies and prototypes of products to meet that market need. In that regard, we were successful. However, neither of us had truly understood the context in which we were working.

We were part of a five-member team that was responsible for developing a portfolio of new products for a market area where we had no current presence. The rest of the team was focused on development of products based on technologies that were currently core to the company. We did not realize that the success of this team depended on successful commercialization of at least one product within a certain time frame. While we had numerous prototypes and customer interest in those prototypes, we did not have a product that was ready for commercialization. The team was disbanded at the end of the year. Despite some key inventions, the two new employees did not realize the context within which our work was ongoing; thus, even though we successfully invented something, we were unsuccessful. Incidentally, the prototypes we invented have not seen further progress. The scenario would have been very different had we had even one product commercialized.

While one can argue that we were new employees and hence the onus for appropriately leading this group and making decisions did not rest with us, the results did affect our careers. Neither of us two new employees did badly but we could have been stars. So we missed being responsible and being part of better decisions. That is a lesson that one needs to take in to the job from day one.

3. *Understanding how you can influence what is expected of you and how you can go about meeting those expectations.* This comment is based on the premise that as a knowledge worker, you are working on complex, nonlinear programs and the true nature of the program will change—the important questions about the program and how you frame it will change—as you delve into the problem. It is therefore necessary to dynamically manage expectations of this effort (What does success mean, when is it achievable, and how is it achievable?) as you begin working on it. It would be a lost opportunity and very foolish not to do so. How do you share this information and continue to define your goals dynamically? Is there even an opportunity to do this?

In the mix of simple, nonlinear and chaotic process that companies typically face, new employees in knowledge worker roles are often unclear how they are performing or how they can improve choices. For an employee who recognizes these classes of problems, opportunities for problem solving and growth present themselves in many ways. This requires dynamic solutions based on scenario analysis and strategic planning using multiple perspectives—an opportunity for a new employee to request support or consulting from numerous experienced colleagues, regular communication, and network building in the process of getting to possible solutions. The new employee should grab this opportunity.

The strategy is one that is generally used in nonlinear problems or chaotic systems—that is, to make a small decision or work a model problem, act in a small way, and then study the response. In an industrial environment, the response must be gathered from all stakeholders and the environment and appropriate communication becomes the most important piece of the solution. This means identifying the true stakeholders and including diversity in the stakeholders in gathering feedback. It also includes understanding the impact on the environment—customers, the industry, or the technical system. One then identifies follow-up strategies, bounces it off stakeholders, and acts a second time. One hopes that through an iteration of such steps with increasing intelligence about the system, one can achieve desired results.

One way to approach this with your supervisor or team leader (as well as with other stakeholders on this program) is to go through an exercise in scenario mapping. Share multiple solutions that you think are possible and go through their implications with him or her. Put together different scenarios presenting the nature of the problem, preliminary results, different strategies based on these results, and different implications after having done your homework on these different strategies and their implications and discuss whether these meet with your expectations. Also discuss what possible ways might be available to measure what you are doing and how it may or may not be valuable as well as when it may be appropriate to bring your role to a close. It might be necessary to do this a few times during the course of your project. This is an effective way to manage your supervisor's and your team's expectations.

It is necessary for you to manage yourself and your projects—that is a prerequisite for you to successfully manage expectations. One way to manage your work is to use a scoring chart for each project, such as the project quad chart shown in Figure 4.1. There are numerous ways you could keep score of each project; this is one. Whatever method you use, it is important that the chart describe the program and how you will implement it, show the context of the program (the business reason you are doing it and why you will win), list the major roadblocks (and your approaches around it), and give an update on where you are with that program. Notice that each of the four sections has underlined comments; they point

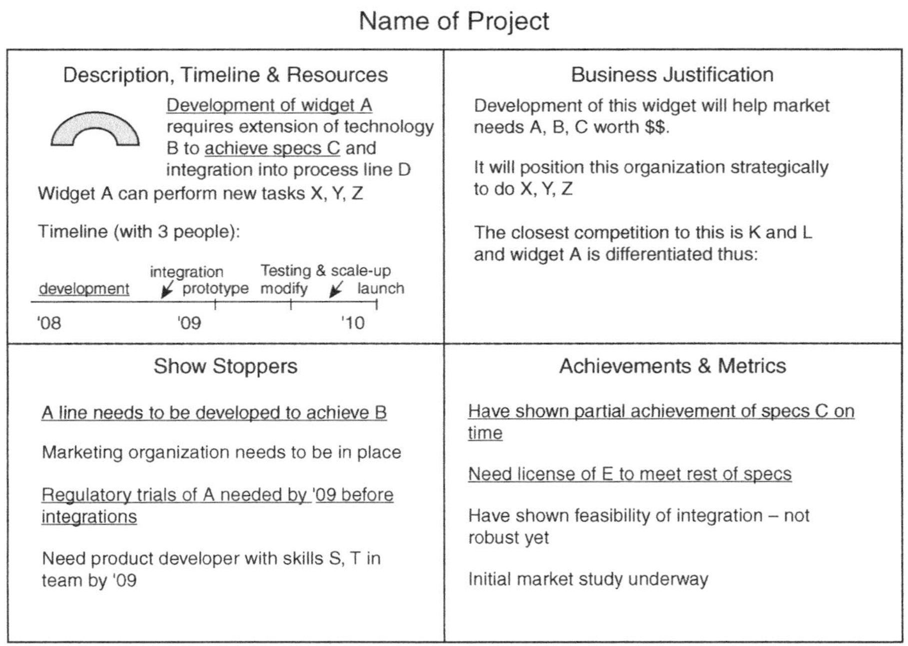

Name of Project

Description, Timeline & Resources

Development of widget A requires extension of technology B to achieve specs C and integration into process line D

Widget A can perform new tasks X, Y, Z

Timeline (with 3 people):

integration   Testing & scale-up
development   prototype   modify   launch

'08   '09   '10

Business Justification

Development of this widget will help market needs A, B, C worth $$.

It will position this organization strategically to do X, Y, Z

The closest competition to this is K and L and widget A is differentiated thus:

Show Stoppers

A line needs to be developed to achieve B

Marketing organization needs to be in place

Regulatory trials of A needed by '09 before integrations

Need product developer with skills S, T in team by '09

Achievements & Metrics

Have shown partial achievement of specs C on time

Need license of E to meet rest of specs

Have shown feasibility of integration – not robust yet

Initial market study underway

FIGURE 4.1. A project quad chart that helps to understand the context of your program, your contributions to it (underlined), and how well you are doing.

out your contributions and the impact of your work (or where you are falling short). After all, you are focused on helping your own career, so keep your focus on your own metrics. It also is a good tool to ensure that the key goals and major hurdles are at the forefront of your plans, and its worthwhile being honest about these because it provides your management a context of how critical your role may be and also provides you the best chance to succeed.

The business motivation clearly states how your work affects the profits of the company, either through increased profits or because it facilitates strategic positioning. It is important to clearly state this since it shows how your efforts align with your primary goal—that is, helping the company make profits. It also helps to lay out what strategies help to protect the gains you will achieve—through new intellectual property, trade secrets, strategic access to market channels, and/or regulatory mechanisms.

Recognizing the needs correctly is perhaps one of the most significant steps toward developing solutions. A close second is developing a strategy that recognizes one's strengths and weaknesses and those of the competition. The upper quadrants in Figure 4.1 describe the needs (business motivation) and the strategy. It is necessary to be honest about the weaknesses of the strategy and to articulate how one can resolve or get around them. That is the purpose of the third quadrant. These weaknesses also change as one builds solutions or as the marketplace changes, and it is important to keep this updated. Articulation of these weaknesses also presents opportunities for you to contribute and show leadership; do not miss these.

The final quadrant provides a metric for the program and for yourself. It is important to list the achievements (yours and the programs) as well as the deadlines missed or attempts that failed. From the perspective of the program and your own growth, it is important to list the impact of these achievements or failure (and the back up strategy if it is the latter). Often, the impact may be more meaningful and quantifiable, especially from a career growth perspective.

As you work through programs and develop a stack of these, it provides a portfolio of your experiences. In some teams you may be the core contributor, in others you might enable the program, and in some others you might lead aspects of the program. Putting these together helps you gain a high-level picture of your own development. Have you led programs? Have you put together successful proposals for projects funded by internal or external agencies? Have you had experience in a number of markets? Have you had roles in different sections of the process of commercializing a product or in specific ones? Are there skills on your strategic career plan that you need to add, and how will you add them? Are you more likely to succeed in certain settings than others? All of these will help you manage your expectations from your own career. It will also help you work with your manager in managing expectations of you.

THE SAME OLD BORING ADVICE

Perhaps the easiest advice to establish yourself is to *work hard, share your results appropriately, and be a person with whom it is pleasant to work*. Half the battle in establishing yourself is won right there. However, it addition to working hard, it is important that you ensure that people recognize you as a key contributor. The impression that people have of you and your contribution affects your performance metrics in the short term and affects your career trajectory in the long term.

One way that you can help people know about your effort is through sharing. Organizations will often have mechanisms for groups to share their learnings or their work. These could include regular updates, opportunities for presentations or at poster sessions, technical reports, or documentary updates. Use these mechanisms effectively. Volunteer to present when possible; it gives people an opportunity to know you and your work. As a new person in an organization, that is a good thing.

If opportunities for presentations are few and far between, develop "working posters" and post them in your workspace. These could be hand-drawn schematics, strategies, and results of a problem you work on. You could add physical prototypes to "working posters" as well. Where it is possible to do this electronically (through websites or blogs or team rooms), do so. For one, these are visual images of your current project and can help you think. You could dynamically make changes to the plan as you go. In addition, it becomes a conversation starter when your colleagues come to your lab. Furthermore, as the working posters change, they provide your peers and your boss an opportunity to see what you are doing. Placing multiple working posters might help present the multiple projects and even their connectedness with each other.

Depending on the culture in your organization, share your work with your peers and get feedback. Share your results and discuss what the implications may be. (However, be judicious; if you run to your peers every time a computer code is successfully compiled, they might begin to avoid you quickly.) Share roadblocks you face, and ask for advice. Discuss your problem—perhaps after you have taken a first shot at a solution—and ask them for different ways that one could solve this. Talk about the kinds of approaches you are taking and whether your peers would prefer one or another, given their experience.

Such conversations are important because they provide opportunities for new employees to share their work with more experienced colleagues—colleagues who know what has been tried in the past or business reasons why some solutions may have failed. They also provide opportunities for new employees to gain credibility and the trust of their peers. Most importantly, it is a smart way of solving problems.

A senior scientist in a large MNC has used a mantra with much success: None of us is as smart as all of us. A best practice he strongly encourages and always uses is this method of real-time dynamic strategizing. After trying to frame the critical issues of a problem and having developed an initial mental model, he shares this with a network of experts who may know about various aspects of the problem. Based on their collective input, he redevelops his mental model and presents an initial strategy of solution, sharing it with this network. Thus, even before he has begun his experiments, he has feedback on how he might want to improve the solution strategy (and he can choose to agree with any input). As he continues to learn more from his work, he continues to pick the brains of a network of experts. In essence, he is using a network of expertise in real time to solve a problem (while those brains are also engaged on their own problems), and any experimental or development plan is optimized across this network of expertise. Besides helping develop most efficient methods in addressing the problem where as many aspects of the problem are being addressed right away as possible, it is also a process where multiple people are also learning real time as the solution progresses—from each other and from the solution itself.

In this discussion of sharing, though, be aware that sharing practices should be based on legal and cultural considerations specific to the organization. For example, there may be intellectual property issues or issues of export control that restrict with whom you can share your work. Also recognize that organizations may have cultures where information flow occurs in very restrictive ways. People may not be comfortable with some mechanisms of sharing. This is not the place to judge those cultures; recognize it and act in a manner that accounts for the local culture.

Another way you show your work ethics is by offering to help, and there will be instances where that opportunity will arise as you share your work. Often, your helping someone with a roadblock or a problem that requires a few hours will bring much benefit. One, it helps you gain credibility and trust and also shows how you work. It is also an opportunity for you to learn from the other person. Two, it shows that you are willing to do what it takes and help beyond your job description. That is significant as you start out your career. (At the same time, do not spend your whole time helping others. After all, your performance will be judged by how well you have performed on your own responsibilities.)

The final piece of advice—be someone with whom it is pleasant to work—seems trite. The advice does not imply that one carry on with an ever-smiling face, nor disagree with anything said, and so on. In knowledge-based jobs that require analysis of complex and chaotic systems, it is imperative that there be disagreement within the team. Being "pleasant to work with" does not require that you not share your concerns or analysis when you disagree with decisions or choices. It implies that you remain respectful and present your perspectives based on appropriate data and analysis of that data. It means that you share credit for success with the whole team.

An important component of your "pleasantness" is communication. Make sure you communicate well with your team. Most people do not like to be surprised with results or with changes in plans. More importantly, people do not like to feel left out when changes happen or new learnings are acquired. If the direction of your program has changed or if you have learned something significantly new, share that information. People value that you continue to share and keep them involved.

During your career—including your initial years—you will experience situations where you will be impacted unfavorably by decisions. These could include decisions about your programs, your promotions, or your annual appraisal. It is quite easy to blow up, to hit out at those making decisions, and so on. However, it only serves to burn bridges; and given the nonlinearity of careers today, that is foolish. Perhaps the best approach is a well-thought-out approach. For one, respect that the person or group making these decisions has nothing personal against you and that, in having to make that decision, he/she made it with his/her best understanding of the scenario. Take the time to put data together that comprise the basis for your disagreement with the decision. Be respectful in sharing this perspective while at the same time being forceful. This approach recognizes that you are in a career (even if you change jobs) for the long haul where you will face difficult decisions. This response also shows your bosses that you are mature and can deal with difficult decisions or situations in a way that is positive while at the same time being forceful. It may not result in the current decision being changed to suit you, but it will certainly add to your value to the company. Any successful leadership is looking to replace itself and nurture new leadership; this approach gives evidence that you react thoughtfully in difficult situations.

SUMMARY

Starting out at a new job requires that you understand the context of your new job and expectations from that job as well as how you will be judged regarding what you deliver and how you do what you are expected to do. A good new employee orientation process will provide much information on these issues that can help you succeed. If such a process does not exist, you can gain the information you need as described in this chapter through key discussions with your manager and team members. It is necessary that you understand your role and expectations of you from your manager and your team members as well; this will help you manage your own role as well as understand how your performance is valued and measured. It will also provide you with the set of parameters that tell you what projects are important and help you start your new job in a way that guarantees success.

KEY TAKEAWAYS

1. Bring your A self to work from the first day. That enthusiasm and commitment will help you engage with the challenges and opportunities that your job throws up. Without such engagement, you cannot grow or establish yourself.

2. Take advantage of your company's new employee orientation processes to learn about the company, its structure, your group, and its goals and how they align with the strategy of the company, its place in the company, key stakeholders, and decision makers in your group. Meet various people in your group and on the teams in which you will work. Begin to learn about the culture of the company, how success is measured, and how the company reacts to risk taking and failure.

3. If the company does not have an adequate orientation program, take the initiative to learn about the group and the company from your manager, your group, team members, and other colleagues.

4. Understand expectations from you, and also understand how you will be measured. Get to know the performance metrics in your company: What are your deliverables and what is considered success, what are different ways to contribute, and what does the company value? Generally, companies will also evaluate

your technical skills, your ability to understand customers and markets and connect them to your function, your communication and collaborative capabilities, your ability and initiative to lead projects and parts of projects, and how you connect to the culture of the organization.

5. It is necessary that you establish yourself as a problem solver early on. In an industrial environment, this means that you recognize problems, scope and define them accurately, and are able to look at the problem holistically, evaluate a variety of solutions, recognize the impact of the problem, and prioritize it, as well as implement the solution. This reputation will help you establish yourself and become an individual who will be approached to solve challenging problems and take on significant opportunities. This is an important aspect of career growth.

6. A key component of starting out in your new job is to get to know your immediate supervisor or manager. What is her management style and what is her philosophy on the goals and strategy of the group? How does she communicate with those who report to her as well as to her own boss? Where is she in her career trajectory? What kind of interaction does she expect with you? This understanding will help you frame your interactions with her, ensuring that you can help her with her role and ensure that she is comfortable with your performance. It will also help your expectations of her— how she will react to things you do and how she will support you.

7. It is also important to know your teams. What are the goals of the teams in which you participate and how are

they aligned with the strategy of the company? What are your roles in each of these teams? How do you prioritize these roles? What is the character of each team? How successful have they been? Who drives the teams—one or two people or the entire team? At what stage of their careers are members of the team? Who are the key stakeholders in the team? What opportunities do you see with each team? Who are the people who best complement your skills? Use this understanding to strategically prioritize your efforts as well as gauge potential roles you might play in each team. Establish yourself by close collaborations on projects that are strategically aligned to company needs.

8. Whether you are considered successful or not depends on what is expected of you. It is important then that you manage expectations from key stakeholders. You do this by understanding your job and responsibilities, the context of your job, and how much you can influence what is expected of you and how you can go about doing that. Based on this, communicate real-time status of all your projects with key stakeholders. This should include scenarios of all your projects based on the nature of the problem, preliminary results, various strategies and their implications along with the context of resources, business needs, external activities, and key challenges. Share ongoing progress and your own expectations from the project defining what *you* think is success.

9. Over time, you can use these project sheets to create your portfolio of programs, analyze your own skill development, identify gaps and opportunities for development or experiences, and also articulate your successes.

10. Connect with your colleagues—through evidence that you are pulling your own weight in your team, helping them with their projects, and sharing knowledge (both what you learn and from their experiences). This connectivity will help you collaborate more effectively as well as help you access help when you need it.

ESTABLISHING YOURSELF

There is much to be learned as a new employee–and that process could take a few months to a year. Concurrently, and quickly, you should also begin to learn about processes, methods, and tools that help you establish yourself in the industry. Beyond learning what your group does, what the focus of your company may be, how your manager operates, and how you manage this relationship, you also need to begin to learn to build and establish your technical expertise, your interaction with people, your collaborative effort, and a strong and effective network. These will sustain your career as well as help you maneuver through opportunities to proactively shape your career.

ESTABLISHING YOUR TECHNICAL CREDENTIALS

Irrespective of whether you are starting in a manufacturing, product development, technical service, quality, or R&D role, establishing yourself as a strong technical person is necessary. It builds your credibility that you understand the technical details of a problem, that you are willing to go into those details

Planning a Scientific Career in Industry: Strategies for Graduates and Academics
By Sanat Mohanty and Ranjana Ghosh
Copyright © 2010 John Wiley & Sons, Inc.

to truly grasp what is happening, and that your decisions are based on such a process. There is implicit understanding that your recommendations and comments have been thought through with appropriate technical consideration. Your co-workers would want you on their teams because they know that you can solve problems. If you eventually are interested in leadership roles, people want you to lead because you will understand their technical difficulties and the choices they make (even if you do not agree with them) and you will make choices based on such understanding. Your first goal on starting your job should be to establish yourself technically.

It is instructive—and unflattering perhaps—to recognize that no mid-sized or large company will ask a new graduate to go solo and address a business critical problem that requires major technology breakthrough or inventions (some smaller companies or start-ups might do that). The problems that new graduates will find themselves addressing in their starting jobs vary from running and maintenance of technical equipment or processes to implementing upgrades to a current product or working on new technology development for longer-term business needs. These problems will be important and challenging, but they will not be anything that another engineer or scientist in the company cannot solve if he had the time.

If you consider this from a manager's perspective, it makes sense. I cannot trust a business critical problem—something that will shut down a factory for even a few hours, delay launch of a major product, or result in major business losses—to someone new and unproven, unless I have no other option. That would be a case of bad management. In addition, if I am hiring a new graduate, I am investing in her success. So I will plan on challenging problems for the graduate—but ones in which she has a strong chance to succeed. This implies that you are being set up to succeed—you only need to work smart.

Different jobs have different work schedules. Some jobs may require you to work on 4–10 different projects over the year. Many will be sequentially scheduled, some might be scheduled in parallel. Other jobs will have you focus on one or two projects through the year—maybe even longer. Try to work on at least two, maybe three, programs during the course of the year—even if one is the primary project and others are side projects. The risk of failure with one project is too high. The project could fail owing to a number of reasons outside your control; or for some reason, you may not do well in that project. Having a few projects increases your probability of success—you have something to show for the year.

You may have situations though, especially if you are in an R&D lab of a large company, where you will be asked to work on one or two long-term programs—programs that do require 18 months or more of sustained research before one can assess the feasibility of the technology and ascertain its market value. At the outset, recognize that the risk of this program is high. As is, you will only know whether this technology is feasible about 12–18 months down the road. That implies that you may have to go through a year with nothing to show—and that is the best-case scenario. Worse, you might go through two years and end up with a project that failed. In an era where companies are being managed quarter to quarter (or even monthly) based on Wall St. feedback, this is riskier today than it was even a decade ago.

As it gets riskier to work on long-term R&D programs, one has to be smarter in strategizing the development of such programs. One can reduce the risk of these long-term techno-logy development programs by considering paths that allow for possible commercialization of intermediate results and technologies that evolve from them.

As an example, consider a modified macromolecular struc-ture of interest to biochemists as described in Figure 5.1. The

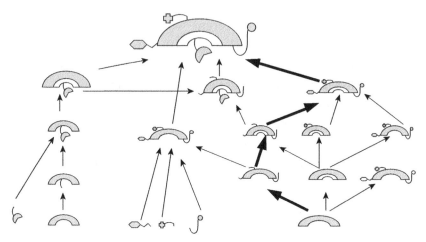

FIGURE 5.1. Technology development pathways to develop a biomolecule.

goal is to develop a new complex bio-macromolecule that has two different surfaces with different properties and specific binding agents (also known as ligands) on each side. The synthesis and characterization of the whole system will probably take a long time, and it is not clear whether the end result will be of any of any commercial interest. Figure 5.1 provides numerous paths to develop such a complex macromolecule. A number of entities are shown as intermediate macromolecules along the path. A strategic program to achieve the goal will be to analyze potential markets for these intermediates. Do they promise some functionality that would be of commercial interest by themselves (or even lead to a different end macromolecule of commercial interest)? The most effective path, you may conclude, is one shown by bold arrows. It may be more effective to start with the outer surface because perhaps it interacts with more systems of interest. Adding the ligands to this system allows for a diverse set of functional groups to be attached subsequently (along with the one of interest to this program). Thus, this intermediate may be of commercial interest, and it can then quickly be used to develop a few other products of interest to the market. Adding the second inner layer to this structure is perhaps an interesting commercial product. The final goal is then a step away. We see from Figure 5.1 that a strategic choice of the pathway for your program can help lower risk of your program and result in multiple other products of interest.

Thus, in achievement of the final goal, you have developed three other entities that were intermediates in this program but by themselves are of commercial interest. Instead of waiting 18 months to show how successful you have been (or know whether you would fail), you now have shown commercially viable products every so often through that period. Even if the final product fails, you have had intermediate successes that were important—the entire project would not have been unsuccessful. In addition, you should remember that all technical inventions do not lead to commercial success and that your primary goal at a company is to help drive growth or enable those who do so. From that perspective, again, you have a greater chance of success in commercialization when you present multiple potential entities that can be commercialized than when you present one.

Of course, there are other reasons why certain paths for technology or product development may not be feasible: Manufacturing using that path may be unfeasible or expensive, there may be blocking intellectual property, and so on. Beware of these aspects as you develop your strategy.

If you are engaged in long-term programs, you might want to consider multiple paths for the goal of your current work—whether it is developing a new technology or a product.[26] Ask yourself what intermediates are possible and who may be interested in these intermediates. Can they be products by themselves or enable other products? Then choose the path forward and develop a timeline when you might have decision

[26] Alternatively, if you are working on short-term programs, ask what else this program could empower across the company.

points for these intermediates. With whom would you need to collaborate to enable these intermediates?

As you start out on such an effort, you will also recognize that you need a strong understanding of the technologies that go into enabling your goals but also need a good understanding of conjugate technologies that might use these intermediates to enable other functionalities, products, or technologies. Thus, effective technology roadmapping requires that you be an expert in technologies and markets that are core to your work as well as have a good understanding of adjacent ones.

In earlier chapters, on numerous occasions we have discussed how your role could affect growth of company in numerous ways (Figure 2.5). In looking through a portfolio of programs (as described in Figure 4.1, for example), you will also recognize that numerous roles and numerous technologies go into making a program successful. Within this context and with respect to technologies, you need to ensure that:

1. You are an expert in one or two areas—you know everything about what is happening globally in this area.
2. In these areas you acquire knowledge about everything that has happened in the company.
3. You acquire an understanding of conjugate areas of expertise.
4. You understand business implications of these technologies.

It is important to understand all critical technologies that are related to your job and to understand the history of these technologies inside your organization and outside. This will help you understand the reasons for certain choices made with respect to this technology as well as the jargon that may be somewhat specific to the area and the company. If your organization has been involved with this technology for a few years already, there will be a wealth of information within the organization that cannot be found outside. This will include interesting variations that were tried, different ways in which the technology was applied, and which ones worked and which ones showed unexpected results as well as what were some key learnings from those results. It is often useful to go through some thought experiments with these historic trials, asking whether things might have been done differently given that technology in contiguous areas has also developed. Would this have led us to some key learnings or applications? The answers may provide opportunities for invention.

In addition, it is necessary to stay abreast of development ongoing in these critical technology areas. With today's internet access, it is quite easy to frequently be updated with abstracts of journal papers from a relevant key word search, keeping up to date on technology developments in your area. Use this information to map which technology and product areas these technology developments might impact and whether there are opportunities and/or threats associated with these developments. Note whether these technology developments applied to your area would result in any small or major breakthroughs. Understand—at least at a high level—what potential business impact this may have for your company. This can become a key document to drive innovation and growth in your area—and build you as the driver of key innovation in your company. Use this document to share your ideas with your colleagues and with your team. Use it as a pin-up in your workspace; it will be one of the best things you could do to begin collaborative interactions with your colleagues who are just beginning to know you and whose trust and respect you need to gain, whose brains and experience you need to tap into.

Also identify major adjacent technologies that are often coupled with the technologies of interest or ones that impact these. While you can be an expert in one or two, to succeed you need to know enough about other roles and technologies that work with yours. That helps appropriate transition of knowledge—you understand better the meaning and implications of what an expert in a conjugate area may be saying. For example, if you are focused on composites technology, you also should be aware of developments in polymer sciences. Or if you are focused on database technologies, you understand that changes in networking capabilities may also affect you. Or if you are modeling environmental phenomena, you should be aware of algorithm development among mathematics and physics communities. Being able to transport learnings across disciplines has historically been a major source of technology development and inventions. You would be missing significant opportunities for success in leaving this out. This analysis also makes sure that you are aware of development in alternative technologies that could make your products or technologies obsolete. It gives you an opportunity to make that shift using strategies that are favorable to you rather than when you are forced to do so. The computer industry has seen a plethora of such instances.

To the above map, it is also wise to add a search of patents in your area of technology. This begins to point out major inventions relevant to the industry. It also begins to highlight the major corporate entities working in this technology area, identifying those who may be competition or potential collaborators or both. The map starts the first steps in competitive analysis and begins to help you understand, perhaps, what strategies are being used by your major competitors or potential collaborators—especially if you superimpose their product platforms on to this map. It also explains to you how competition is using key technology developments for new product growth as well as alliances they continue to develop to win in this market. You begin to understand where your competition may be going, what technologies they are using to strengthen their positions, and how you should strategize to win—all through ethical processes. It also begins to help you identify potential collaborators and understand how it fits into your strategy to win.

This set of analysis provides you with the context within which relevant set of technologies and products are placed. It gives you both direction and justification for technology and product development and for growth, and it provides the data and analysis you can use to do so.

Your success in the program depends on your plans that adapt to dynamic external realities. As you plan your program and as you choose strategies to address the problems, meditate on the shorter-term and longer-term impact of these choices. Of course, if you are trying to resolve an issue within 24 hours or even a week and you have to find whatever works and make it go, this option does not exist. However, if you have some time to choose technical tools or strategize on a solution, ask whether this set of tools or strategy will result in other nearer- or longer-term successes or breakthroughs or even minor advantages. Ask whether the tools you choose strategically add on to the technology toolbox or expertise or whether they draw from the core. Both of these may be good ideas, depending on the context—but it is important to highlight and articulate them. Will there be intermediate prototypes or solutions that could result in new products or make a commercial impact in another way? Building such a plan helps to improve your overall probability of success.

Another component of your portfolio might to be a self-driven project, even at 5–10% of your time. This is not possible in all work situations. The project should be based on a need you perceive that requires you to develop tools or technologies that do not exist. In essence, the goal of this project is to leapfrog current development plans. Often, technology develops in some incremental or linear sense. This self-driven program attempts to predict what the trajectory of this progression might be and get there before the business, the markets, or the industries do. Thus, you will be a solution leader when that happens—a great way to strengthen your credibility. The program, as mentioned earlier, might be focused on tool development as relevant to your job. Perhaps you see that a certain tool does all right but that with growing complexity of the solutions in the industry, the current tool may become cumbersome. This might be a software tool, a process line, or an analytical tool, for example. Of course, the added advantage of this is that you could work on something about which you are passionate.

You could independently use such a program to develop skills that you need as per your career strategy analysis. It could also become a vehicle to connect with groups or businesses in your organization that you are otherwise unable to connect with—and those that you value as strategic. Along the same lines, you could use this as a vehicle to build credibility in an area to help you move to another organization that you value— as long as you are aware of transfer of intellectual property with such a move.

A researcher at an R&D lab told the story of such a side project. For one simulation project that she was assigned to, the team needed to develop models of various transportation systems to understand how they could minimize fuel costs. The team used a certain type of modeling tool that was geared toward transportation systems to build this model. It was a complex tool that required a nontrivial learning curve. In another project, she needed to model a supply chain system to maximize its efficiency and had to use another modeling tool for this, which had an associated learning curve as well. She could see the benefits of using very specific learning tools built for specific domains, but the learning curves of each of them made the team lose precious time each time a domain changed. She got together with a few more colleagues to develop a generic domain modeling framework that could be easily used for a

*variety of domains and could be tailored for a specific domain
as well.*

*This started off as a small side project and ended up being a crude
yet handy tool, which a number of other teams started using as well,
saving them significant amounts of development time. This tool
started getting the attention of managers in the lab. They saw the
value of this tool and gave more resources to her and her collaborators
to build a more sophisticated version of it. This side project brought her
and her team a lot of recognition and built a huge amount of credibility
for them in the company.*

COMMUNICATION AND COLLABORATION

Development of strategies and their effective implementation
in day-to-day operations are based on information that the
company gathers, in different ways and formats. The effectiveness of a company depends on how well it is able to bring critical
pieces of information together to make decisions and act on
them. Communication and collaboration are thus two critical
aspects for a company's effective operation. In considering your
own job, you will notice that you gather information from
different sources, analyze it, and then communicate this to
others to help catalyze specific action or act yourself. How
effective you are in the totality of these describes how well you
function. Communication and collaboration are thus key to
your own career.

Effective communication is the basis of keeping a company
going so that it will meet its goals—irrespective of whether you
work in R&D, product development, manufacturing, or customer services. Companies value it enough to offer numerous
courses in effective communication. They realize that given the
scale of its operations, numerous people need to be *working
together* to efficiently make profits. A company recognizes that
operating in a market space that requires innovation in different

forms (technical, design, manufacturing, marketing) is a non-linear process at the very least and its employees must act in ways that leverage each other for success. Information—not just data—must efficiently make its way across hierarchies to groups that need that information and that will make decisions based on it or act on it. Analysis of those decisions (or that information) must also efficiently be transmitted across the company to specific groups or people. This requires effective communications, and companies attempt to build a culture of effective communications and skills that go with it.

Excellent books already exist on effective communication[27,28] in the workplace, and we recommend these. It would be outside the scope of this discussion to lay out all aspects of effective communication (and we are not experts in this area). Our focus is to help the new employee understand the role of communication in being effective at your job as well as pointing out aspects of communication that could help you grow.

While the archetypal scientist is portrayed to be a reserved, taciturn moody individual, a modern technology-based organization can ill accommodate such an individual. If you do not gather key information (for example, customer needs, market strategy, manufacturing constraints, raw material changes) from different parts of the organization as inputs for your work, what you do may be of little use to the organization. In addition, if you do not share your resulting analysis, it hinders information flow and affects the effectiveness of your position.

One senior scientist recognized early on that his oral communication skills were poor. He usually became very passionate

[27]P. S. Perkins and Les Brown, *The Art and Science of Communication: Tools for Effective Communication in the Workplace*, Wiley, 2008.

[28]*Harvard Business Review on Effective Communication*, Harvard Business School Press, 1999.

about what he was saying and would either digress from what he intended to say or say things he wished he would not have said. During presentations, he became so nervous that he completely lost the complex nuances of the story. But he was a very good scientist who had help grow his organization by over 500 million dollars net worth during his career. He achieved effective communication by disciplining himself to send written communications to everyone with whom he wanted to communicate before he spoke with them orally. During presentations, his audience had often received his presentation with substantial annotation before the event. In addition, he had a number of cue cards that he used. He shared his weakness openly with his colleagues—they were eager to support him through these endeavors.

From the perspective of the above discussion, what roles does communication play in your job (and more generally in your organization)?

1. It helps you get information about different aspects of internal operations and external trends that affect your project. You can get some of the information passively—where key stakeholders provide such information. However, there is much information needed for your project that you must systematically research to find out who has knowledge, what their own motivations and plans may be, and what they can share.

2. It helps you connect with other members working on the same project or similar projects, and it enables you to collate activities, learnings from these activities, and their implications. It helps you take advantage of the groups' collective wisdom and experience and decide on your collective strategy. It then helps provide direction to specific activities that each member must undertake to implement and further that strategy.

3. It helps you connect with key stakeholders and understand what they want from you and your project. As trends change and new information evolves, how do they see the need for your project and its deliverables change? How do they view your strategy and plans? What information are you getting from them vis-à-vis trends and changes at a high level? What pressures do they feel with respect to your project? And what feedback do you get from them? At the same time, what are you telling your stakeholders? What do you need from them? When do you need them to be your advocate? How are you managing this relationship to help launch and sustain your project and its deliverables?

Essentially, communication facilitates these key aspects of your job. While you still have to deliver to be successful, good communication helps you get all the information you need to make the right decisions, share the knowledge with your team, and plan appropriately and then prepare key decision makers appropriately to help the launch of your deliverables. Without it, your efforts are not grounded in context and the risk of failure becomes higher.

Within a work environment, communication thus serves a key purpose. The tools that allow for effective communication are also quite straightforward. Essentially, they are ways for one individual with a certain need and a certain personality (in terms of the format and kind of information with which they resonate) to connect with another individual with perhaps a different need and a different personality. As a new employee, this can be an effective basis to build your communication tool set.

An organization will usually have people with different levels of comfort in communicating. There are those who are least interested in interacting with anyone. They are often forced to minimal communication to be part of a "supply chain" of information. They only want to know what needs to be done and will pass on information about what was done and its implications as necessary. While what they do may be of significant impact to the company, at this level of communication it is difficult to leverage that impact when they are not engaged in working with others to change things to take advantage of what you learned. The stereotypical "grumpy scientists," for example, do extremely well at "leave me alone and I will do what I need to do" but face difficulty growing because of their unwillingness (not inability) to communicate more effectively.

Communication at the second level requires dynamic (reevaluate knowledge following actions based on feedback and respond with the newer understanding) and real-time (share as you do this, not after a week or a month) sharing of information and knowledge. This requires more interactions with people. Depending on the nature of the projects and their goals, this might require interactions every 15 minutes or, perhaps, every week. Those engaged in this level of communication are often technology or product developers who interact freely with their peers. They recognize that feedback such as this requires them to constantly reevaluate their analysis. It also pushes their knowledge and understanding and they enjoy this. It helps them grow intellectually (and they thrive on it) and promises career growth. Communication at this level requires them to somewhat understand what each of their colleagues does so that they understand the knowledge base from which the colleague provides input. It also requires them to understand the motivations of their colleagues so they can connect with the context of their work.

At another level, there are people who want to understand the needs of stakeholders or leaders invested in making decisions and providing them with strategies that meet those goals based on data and analysis from your research. At this level of communication they are not only sharing information about what they are doing or how they are collaborating, they are in fact using that knowledge to influence strategies based on an insight into the needs of stakeholders. Often, these transcend purely technical communities and are at the interface of technical and business needs. While there are technical people who do not enjoy such communication and shy away from them, there are others who enjoy the complexity and the grayness of such communication and decision making.

Understanding the comfort level of your colleagues in these kinds of communication can help you communicate with them. Understanding your own interest and comfort levels can help you chart your career strategy as well. These levels of effective communication are based on your willingness to engage in shaping the shared space, primarily through an understanding of needs and the development of shared strategies that meet a set of diverse needs. Effective communication, thus, becomes the bedrock of good leadership.

Different people in the same company have different motivations and needs. They may have varied influences which include:

1. The organization in which they reside and how it is measured (for example, an R&D organization will be measured different from a manufacturing organization, which will be different from a marketing organization).

2. Specific forces that may be acting on their organization or trends that may influence them differently (for example, one organization may be more exposed to a certain market that is changing rapidly and hence people in that organization are focused on reacting to that market and cannot be bothered about anything else).

3. Past experience (for example, one individual has found it difficult to work with a certain organization and will not

want to repeat that experience, or a group knows from past experience that a certain tool has specific strengths and weaknesses and will base their decisions on that experience even if other data suggest otherwise).

4. Personal situations (for example, one individual may be focused on being part of a commercialization team because she knows it is a prerequisite to her next promotion, or another may want to use a certain tool as opposed to any other since he invented that tool).

In interacting with individuals to achieve your goals—to get information, to collaborate, or to build support—you will have to spend the time to understand their motivations and needs that are relevant to your project. How do they see your program? What needs does it serve, and what value does it provide? What potential solutions are most favorable, and what tools would they recommend? Have similar projects been tried in the past, and what were key learnings? What potential hurdles do they see in implementation and success of the project? Such a discussion would help you understand the interest and motivation of another person and hence shape your communication with that person.

Such information would be useful as you shape your project. In addition, your communication with this individual should be focused on aligning his or her motivations with the needs of the program. For example, if you and your team have analyzed information and decided that this project should use a certain tool whereas this individual believes that a different tool should be preferred, the goal of your communication is well-defined. Or if your team has concluded that the goal of this project should serve a certain customer base while this individual believes that such a customer base does not bring value to your organization, the goal of your communication is clear. It is important to note that some initial work is often required to identify the goal of communicating with specific individuals— this may require some research. How much effort should go into such an effort depends on the importance of this individual to your effort.

While knowing that the goal of communicating with another individual or group is important, the methods and tone you use in communicating is also important. To the extent that communication is about sharing of information and synthesis of ideas, methods of communication include verbal, visual, written, and use of prototypes and working models, among others. Often we restrict ourselves to use of one or two of these, but most experts agree that these are most effective when a few of them are used to complement each other. We usually learn through multiple modes, and use of multiple means of communication helps to engage all those modes.

The tone of your communication is also important. You will probably use different techniques with an executive, your boss, and a peer. You may also use different methods, depending on what you are trying to achieve. You may use different methods, depending on the personality of the individual.[29] Even with the same individual during the same conversation, you might use different methods and tones – changing from logic and analysis to personal and emotional and from pleading to arguing. There are many books on negotiating strategies[30] and communication methods—suffice to say that the more communication tools you have and use, the more effective you will be at communicating.

[29]Significant research (such as on Myers–Briggs techniques) show that different personalities respond to different kinds of communication styles and that effective communication styles should be based on understanding these differences in people. http://epublications.bond.edu.au/cgi/viewcontent.cgi?article=1026&context=hss_pubs.

[30]*Harvard Business Essentials Guide to Negotiation*, Harvard Business School Press, 2003.

As a new employee, you will be most involved in collaborative efforts—and that will perhaps be the location of most of your communication. You will find that good collaboration rests on good communication, and the discussions above will be relevant to your efforts in collaboration. You will recognize that collaboration is a process of shared evolution and implementation of ideas—good communication allows you to build and sustain that shared space. You will also recognize that maintenance and sustenance of that shared space becomes even more difficult in global and diverse teams where individuals and organizations have greater differences in motivations, needs, and cultural norms. Good communication practices become even more critical.

Working in global teams is challenging, not only from a logistical view (coordinating time zones, busy calendars, etc.), but also from a collaboration standpoint. A team working on a major product offering spanned across several countries. A version of the product was released in June, and another version was scheduled for release in December. The development, integration, testing, marketing, and program management teams were all in different locations. The marketing team had promised the customers several new features in the December release and worked with the program management team to lay out a schedule for incorporating those new features. Over teleconferences (held at odd hours, due to time zone differences), the development team was given instructions on what needed to be done and by when.

In November of that year, the project suddenly went into a panic mode, due to several reasons. There was a major holiday season at one of the locations at the end of October to early November, during which time a lot of team members were on vacation. In another location, many team members had vacation plans for the December holiday season. The teams realized they had not accounted for these differing vacations schedules in their plans. In addition, the teams realized that major design changes needed to be incorporated to include some of the required features. The integration and testing teams required more than the allocated one month to complete their end of the job. It was clear that the December deadline would not be met. There was growing frustration between teams located remotely from each other.

The deliverable had to be delayed and the product was not released until the end of March. The company lost face with its customers. This resulted in a blame game between teams and team members. The situation became ugly, and upper management had to intervene; several people were moved out of the program.

It is quite easy to see that there was breakdown of communication between teams in this project. Timelines were too aggressive for such major changes in the project, but no one provided that feedback during planning. The development teams did not convey their concerns to the other teams early enough in the program. The integration and testing teams accepted the schedule that was dictated to them during the teleconferences and thought they would be able to accomplish their tasks, without communicating to the program management team that they would need more time. No one brought up the fact that people in various countries traditionally take vacations during certain times of the year. The program management team did not understand the implications of the holiday season in different locations and convey that to the marketing team, asking them to review either the deadline or the new features. All teams waited until the last moment to tell the others that things were not going well.

On the face of it, the teams appeared to be communicating regularly: There were weekly teleconferences and regular emails. But there was no effective communication. No one wanted to convey bad news or appear to be the cog in the wheel, so many important concerns were not voiced. Culturally, some teams thought they needed to do as told and hence did not speak up. Also, the management team did not try to understand real issues faced by the different teams. The teams were not effectively collaborating as parts of a whole; rather they were operating as independent fragments, with their own individual goals.

A year after this incident, some of the team leaders did meet up and introspect over these failures. A lot of damage was done to this program, but it did offer a good case study for these team members and others throughout the company on what not to do in a collaborative effort.

Effective communication is the bedrock of a strong team and of good collaboration. It requires numerous individuals to communicate at a high level of leadership to create and sustain a shared space (discussed in the earlier section) that empowers the team to achieve its goals. We have already discussed at length the need for strong teams in industrial organizations. In his book *Organizing Genius*, Warren Bennis[31] presents six case studies including the 1992 Clinton Campaign, the Disney animation studio, the Manhattan Project and the making of USA's atom bomb, Xerox's PARC labs, and the legendary Skunk Works to show the collaborative advantage of powerful and committed teams and how well-managed collaborative programs can beat the most driven individual efforts. This section explores some key aspects of collaborative programs and the dynamics of successful teams, laying emphasis on your role in building strong teams. At the outset, though, one should recognize that most teams are not driven or empowered like the teams that Bennis describes—numerous factors need to coincide for such teams to evolve. Most teams have their conflicts and fractious elements. This section will also discuss strategies to be successful with such teams.

One caveat before we embark on this discussion – teams and team dynamics are topics that need much in-depth discussion as books by Bennis and numerous others suggest. One section can hardly do justice to such a topic. The goal of this section is modest: It attempts to describe how teams in industrial settings

[31]W. Bennis and B. Nanus, *Leaders: The Strategies for Taking Charge*, Harper and Row, New York, 1985.

might be understood and then points out some characteristics of ideal teams and some working models to a new graduate joining the industry.

Teams in industrial organizations are built to deliver specific program goals. They are built of people of diverse backgrounds who bring specific skills sets, experiences, or access to specific resources. Real-world (and industrial) teams are different from teams in an academic setting (such as those that come together to write a paper or a proposal) in two major ways: (1) The implications of success or failure are often more serious or significant. (2) The nature of the problems usually require engagement of more complex sets of skills and functional responsibilities.

In the examples that Bennis describes in his book, most of these teams were made up of people who had dedicated all their time and energy to the goals of their teams. In usual industrial organizations and teams, this is unfeasible and unsustainable. How, then, can one understand teams that are more real and ones we will experience? There are some key features of any team that defines it. While this is not an exhaustive list, discussion along these parameters can help think through the dynamics of your own team:

1. *Its members believe in themselves.* They believe that they have the ability to gather and analyze knowledge, learn skills, and act based on that knowledge using those skills. Each member of the team has key roles and respects himself or herself as a key contributor. If they do not have the expertise necessary, they believe they can access and acquire knowledge in the field to solve any problem. In addition, each member of the team has the motivation and discipline to do what needs to be done to solve the problem. These highly talented people must realize that in today's world it is necessary to work in teams, to collaborate to achieve success.

Many teams, however, have some significant number of people who are either not experts or are not motivated or disciplined to do what it requires to solve the problem. If there is a majority of such people, the project starts at a disadvantage. If one such person is assigned key responsibility within the team, the project starts at a disadvantage. The team usually ends up dragging these dead weights along. These can, however, be overcome if a significant number of people are able to step up and contribute beyond their "fair share." Quite early, though, the team needs to recognize this and work through these concerns.

In addition, if there are even a few people who do not want to play with others, it can become a serious problem; the team spends a significant amount of time mollycoddling—or ignoring internal distractions—but the team can be successful through effective communication and well-thought-out program planning. As an individual, it is most important that you not be one such person. It is possible to find responsibilities that allow for smaller overlap with such people who do not wish to play with others; and if forced to, one can still succeed by managing the expectations of the team leader while also working on effective communication with your teammates. Such communication needs to allow for sharing of strategies that meet their needs (that perhaps drive this unwillingness to play with others) while meeting your needs of fulfilling your responsibilities and personal goals.

2. *The condition of intellectual equality exists.* It ensures that intellectual questions are not defined by the experience or position of the person but by the question itself. Most members of the team recognize that the problem is complex and that new areas may have to be explored that may lie outside well-defined expertise. In addition, team members understand that they are in this not just as experts in an area but as highly talented

problem solvers. This understanding implies that members of the team are intellectual equals and will cross hierarchies, functional boundaries, and predefined roles to get the job done. It implies that the seriousness in addressing the question is also unaffected by the position of the person. It is also necessary that individuals be able to cross boundaries of organization, expertise, and hierarchies; this ensures that solutions include all perspectives from the group, not just the biases of an expert. These ground rules result in the team taking ownership of a problem and also result in members being engaged in differing degrees with all aspects of the problem. It also implies that new problems, as they arise, get the attention of the team and are addressed through enthusiastic volunteering of one or more individuals who think they can best solve this problem and guided by a breadth of expert perspectives.

Many teams are not set up this way, and this is usually a reflection of the need to keep egos secure through marking out territories where experts feel that they are not to be questioned. Such boundaries effectively end a truly collaborative effort and stymie creative solutions that could arise from the meeting of disciplines and the interstices of expertise. (It is interesting to note that most new inventions and breakthroughs continue to occur in such interstices.) One way around this—though of limited implications—is to find a group of individuals who are willing to work through such a truly collaborative process and form a subteam that addresses the responsibilities of the members in a collaborative fashion. This may be easier said than done if the responsibilities of these willing members do not naturally overlap. However, it is an exercise worth pursuing.

It is important to note that this mode of collaboration truly requires the creation of a shared space where people feel empowered and not insecure. Communication plays a key role in establishing and maintaining—even growing—this space. Since the team is focused on addressing complex problems, it should assume that numerous technology breakthroughs and inventions will be required to achieve its goals and that these will be in areas that transcend one or more predefined domains of knowledge. Thus, numerous problem solvers with a breadth of expertise will have to engage with the problem in a wide variety of ways. Second, since these are complex problems with a solution that cannot be predetermined, one cannot *a priori* demand that individual x be charged with inventing certain technologies, or even that certain steps will lead to breakthroughs. All one can do is take steps based on scientific analysis—as behooves a chaotic or indeterminate problem—and reevaluate based on observations or results from those steps. This requires constant engagement, critique, and reevaluation. There is no space for feudal domains or egos within the team. Only effective communications (and a commitment by all team members) can ensure such a safe space.

3. The *presence of the safe space*. There is usually some tension in successful teams. Often these are teams that are pushing frontiers of knowledge or of what can be done. There are aspects of unknown and multiple ideas of what can be done. And there are numerous leaders and experts engaged and participating as equals and team members. If there is no tension and if everyone agrees on everything (even most things), then something is not right. There should be tension in the team – tension between ideas, between potential paths forward. It is unhealthy and counterproductive to end this tension by annihilating opposing perspectives. The presence of the safe space—well announced and made sacrosanct—can ensure that such tension contributes positively to the team and the achievement of necessary goals.

Sometimes leadership tramples on such tension by getting rid of members with opposing ideas. Such leadership often results in breakdown of all the other guidelines described here for the formation of strong and successful teams. In such situations, your role may depend on your relationship with the leadership and with the rest of the team. At the very least, it should include confidential or informal discussions with team members about what alternative methods you could use to fulfill your responsibilities. You could broaden that to even identifying some "safer" or less controversial aspects of the program and exploring a variety or methods to resolve those aspects. This will certainly help you follow the best possible solution in a limited fashion. It might help exemplify the advantage of such analysis that takes advantage of numerous ideas, some that are contradictory or in tension.

4. *A team of leaders.* The style of leadership is not predetermined—it is certainly not top down—but is designed for the group. The only role of a leader is to help the team achieve its objectives. The leadership attempts to facilitate resources, communication, and roles to ensure that the shared space is sacrosanct and the team achieves its goals. At the very onset, the team leadership must recognize that this is in fact a team of leaders and that each individual is trying to push and pioneer in ways that allow for the team to succeed. Such leaders are often intrinsically mavericks—they certainly are not obedient and they did not become successful by following orders. The role of the team leader is not to threaten or counter the leadership of the members. Its role is to ensure that the leadership of a member does not affect the leadership of another—again maintaining the shared space. The leader of such a team does not usually have to worry about critical jobs not being done. If the team is engaged with the problem and owns it, then what is needed to be done will be done. The leader plays a more administrative role, without being a bureaucrat. The leader

ensures that the team has the resources (and access to key decision makers) it needs to succeed while at the same time buffering the team from distractions. In addition, the leader ensures that key milestones are being met (and this is where the leader must not be a bureaucrat). The leader recognizes that decisions must be made—since a group of such individuals may not necessarily be decisive—and will help make decisions. In playing this role, the leader must remember that she is not a general or a dictator but a facilitator and help make decisions without being *ad hoc* or arbitrary but through a process to which the team may have agreed and is data-driven.

Often, while the team members and the team dynamics is not ideal, neither is the leadership. The leader may use more traditional styles of leadership and play the role of a director rather than a facilitator. Such a hurdle is more difficult to overcome—it usually requires that team members manage their leader through intensive communication, sharing of data, analysis, and scenario mapping. The "leader" can also become a millstone that pulls the team down, ironically.

5. In addition, the *team should share the dream* or be committed to the collective goals. While this may be an ideal—and may even be feasible when team members are completely and exclusively committed to one program—in the real world where individuals may be working on multiple programs with more immediate deadlines and results, this is often not true. Under these circumstances, it becomes more practical to tie the success of the program with needs of a team member and their own success. Managing such a diverse set of motivation should be the responsibility of the team leader; however, if there are lacunae in the fulfillment of such responsibilities, someone in the team should step up. As a new graduate, this might be a difficult task for you to accomplish; however, it is possible through communication with your team once you have established your credibility.

6. *Implementation and the discipline to get things done.* Great teams are not just thinkers or philosophers; they have to be able to get to what they plan to achieve. They are not idea hoppers (pun intended). They are dreamers, but not *just* dreamers. They focus on what needs to be achieved. They learn to act and deliver with a variety of constraints, including the constraint of time. They are creative enough to transcend the constraints of time, often of resources, sometimes of limited data as well as the constraints of team dynamics.

Often, teams (or certain sections of a team) tend to procrastinate waiting for all the data or for the perfect equipment. That requires members of the team to take the initiative to develop analysis and scenarios that allow for the team to move forward.

We share some key learnings from a study by Linda Graton and Tamara J. Erickson[32] on the "right conditions" for effective collaboration among teams. In the context of their study, they found that in today's work environment, most industrial teams had the following characteristics (irrespective of whether they succeeded or not)— characteristics that perhaps define the nature of our work and the nature of the problems that are to be solved:

1. *Teams are larger today than they were two decades ago. They have to be larger to (a) include the interest of multiple stakeholders, (b) include a wider set of skills necessary to solve the problem, and (c) account for a diverse set of activities. While sociological and behavioral studies show that teams become less effective as the number of individuals grow beyond a critical number (15–20), today's teams have to succeed with a larger number of team members.*

2. *The teams are more diverse to ensure that broader sets of skills and expertise can be brought to bear on the problem. However,*

---

[32]L. Graton, T.J. Erickson, "Eight Ways To Build Collaborative Teams", Harvard Business Review, November 2007.

increasingly these are teams of people who have rarely met; and, given the need for quick solutions, these teams are quickly put together and asked to perform. Studies show that people who hardly know each other and have different backgrounds are less likely to share data or trust results, analysis, or decisions.

3. *In an increasingly global workplace, more teams have virtual interactions. This has become necessary because the skills are globally located. In addition, often the problem and/or the solution has global implications and hence global stakeholders need to be involved. When teams do not meet in real space, collaborations suffer.*

4. *Increasingly, teams are made up of highly educated individuals with narrowly defined but highly specialized fields of expertise. Studies have shown that as the number of experts grows in a team, collaborative output suffers and there is greater incidence of dissipative conflicts.*

Within this context, the above authors set out to identify what made some teams collaborate more effectively than others. They found that:

1. *The behavior of senior leadership made a significant impact on the culture of collaboration in the company. Teams in companies where a senior executive was seen to collaborate made more of an effort to do so as well. The leadership provided a role model and held their own behavior as the standard for the rest of the company to match. Best practices in collaboration were more effectively permeated through the company. In addition, whether leadership made tangible efforts to facilitate collaboration also mattered. Companies that were structured organizationally or physically (through facilities) to interact more showed more effective collaboration. Practices to encourage more face-to-face interaction—even if that meant greater travel costs—helped effective collaboration. Collaboration was also*

more effective in companies where the leadership made the effort to mentor and train less experienced colleagues—a practice that also then permeated across the company. This "gift" of mentorship was valued by the mentees as valuable to their own growth and helped better relational skills as well as building of informal networks to help employees get to know more people and be more effective.

2. Human Resource organizations of companies were also seen to play an important role in helping effective collaborative practices. Companies that recognize that skills required for effective collaboration are ones that transcend technical expertise and then help their HR provide those skills were companies that significantly improved effective collaboration. Such skills include social, communication, and emotional skills such as how to negotiate, how to work through conflicts, or how to influence others. In addition, collaboration was also high in companies where strong communities had been built—such as communities of women professionals, or those around certain hobbies. HR could help facilitate setting up of such communities.

3. Team structure was also an important parameter affecting success of teams. Researchers have found that teams where a significant fraction of the team know each other or have collaborated effectively in the past often have a better chance to succeed. The team builds on the positive experiences and relationships that these individuals already have. In addition, it was also important that members of the team had clearly defined roles with flexibility in how they decided to fulfill these roles. In the absence of role clarity, too much time is spent on conflicts around turf wars. In addition, when the roles are clearly defined and the method of fulfilling the goals is left open-ended, team members are more willing to engage with each other in getting to those goals. Finally, if not unexpectedly, the choice of the team leader is critical. Studies suggest that

individuals who can manage both task and relationship aspects of a team or a program are more effective in leading the team: They manage how the program progresses while at the same time making sure that relationships necessary for the program to progress are in a good state.

It seems that all studies point to better management and more company-wide initiatives to help more effective collaboration within teams. How does it empower a new graduate starting at an entry-level position—hardly one that wields much management authority? To understand effective collaboration and how teams should ideally perform, seeing—or reading about—some of the best teams is a good place to start. It is necessary that a new employee understand the dynamics of a team within the context of its goals as well as understand the nuances of how people within the team interact. It is critical that a new employee understand the nature of interactions—social, emotional, and political—that provide the framework for technical information shared, decisions made, and the level of trust in those decisions. Case studies such as these provide the benchmark that helps the new employee understand her own experiences within team settings and discriminate between what works and what does not.

Beyond serving as longer-term coaching opportunities, these studies also provide shorter-term opportunities for the new employee. It helps a new employee understand that at the very least, an industrial team requires more than the individual's technical competence. It requires his social and emotional energy as well. For example, while an individual might be required to own a certain component of a team's responsibility—and might be showing good progress—it is not enough for the individual to share that information at the end of the timeline. With team goals often being interdependent, it is necessary for individuals in a team to share information at regular frequency. Not doing so will cause the individual to be labeled as "not a team player." Thus, a new employee needs to understand how often he should share his progress in a productive manner, and are there some who need to know more often and in greater detail than others.

Similarly, a new graduate also needs to learn about communicating as a team and communicating for the team. Often, various stakeholders will request updates, and they may approach a team member for updates on a specific aspect. While it is "legal" for the individual to respond to the stakeholder with an update, doing so unilaterally may be socially inappropriate. Often, teams manage expectations from programs by controlling information going out of the team. Sometimes, they also control information flow to establish IP advantages or export control laws. In addition, sometimes, a group leader would need to know how the team is interacting with various stakeholders to ensure that the message shared is consistent. Unilateral notes—even if the sender included only those aspects of progress that the team agreed on—could cause some stress within the team. One way to avoid such problems is to build good personal relationships with specific members of the team so that they can coach you on what works and what does not within this team and so that if and when you make such mistakes, they are willing to give you the benefit of doubt and work with you to sort it out. Besides avoiding such problems, understanding of how effective teams work can also provide you with opportunities to succeed. At a personal level, it is important to recognize that as a new employee, while you have to build your credibility, you also do not have any baggage. No one has any problems or preconceptions in interacting with you. Since these studies all show the importance of good relationships, it is necessary that you build good relationships with some of the key people in the team as well as good working relationships with all. Through these relationships, it is important to understand protocols for sharing information, making decisions, and resolving differences in opinions.

Most of all, though, this helps a new graduate calibrate the team(s) in which he participates. What are the rules of engagement? Is it a team who believes in itself? Is it a team that shares the goals and dreams embodied in the project? Are all members engaged? Is there intellectual equality or is there a clear hierarchy? Who are key stakeholders and how can she engage with and influence decisions of the team? Is there a safe space, where those with opposing opinions can go at it without egos being bruised and self-esteem decimated? Will the team make decisions based on objective analysis of ideas?

One of the toughest tasks for a new employee is to navigate the organization and the teams within which she operates. A framework for good collaboration lays down the parameters through which to view any team—and hence the map to navigate through, around, or away from teams.

A manager in an R&D laboratory of a corporation that focused on developing consumer goods described a new employee who joined them from one of the best research groups in the United States. He came highly recommended with a strong body of published work in the area; clearly he knew his area well and had made significant contributions to the science in his area and had a strong work ethic. When he started working, though, his team members complained to the manager that this person did nothing and did not share any information. He came to group meetings without anything to share, said very little, and left at the end of the meeting. The manager was concerned.

Through her discussions though, she discovered that the new employee was actually working very hard. However, in his academic research group, it was considered inappropriate to present half-done work, and even obnoxious to present preliminary work without having worked through the details of the idea. When he joined this team, given that it was a different enough area, he had spent time learning about it, formulated some ideas of how to develop the field, and was working on it. He did not deem it appropriate to offer opinions or share his preliminary results in team meetings; he even thought that people might think that he was being arrogant if he did so. He had not realized that the team dynamics and needs from individuals were very different in an industrial environment. Thus, his ignorance of the social dynamics and team needs threatened the project itself as well his own reputation and career.

While he had joined the team with remarkable technical expertise, clearly his social intelligence was underdeveloped. Even though he had worked in "teams" in an academic setting, they did not require real time sharing of plans and data in the same way. In addition, he did not notice that other team members were sharing preliminary information (even if they made it sound as if they knew everything about it), nor did he recognize that the development of the product and achievement of team goals depended on real time sharing of information and plans. Coaching was necessary to help the individual truly understand the functioning of a team and become part of the team.

For the team, it is important to define the common goals as well as processes that are well-defined and shared so that the team can be effective without constantly coming to conflicts. You could help reinforce this shared space by taking on simple tasks—such as documenting extensively all discussions and decisions, maintaining lists of choices and tasks (as politically appropriate), or even setting up regular meetings. Even such seemingly menial tasks help to define and direct team dynamics and effectiveness while at the same time helping you build tenure as a new employee. With time, you will find that such steps allow you to transition into influencing decisions or defining choices more easily.

BUILDING NETWORKS

A senior manager from a pharmaceutical company told us about his career and the significance of networks. He was a rising star in his company, leading a laboratory that served its business unit by developing new formulations. He had a very strong network with his counterparts leading marketing, manufacturing, and regulatory functions. For three years, the team had been very successful in developing new formulations including a couple of blockbusters. Besides highly talented and committed people in the laboratory, a critical component of this success was his network with his counterparts; this relationship ensured that all sections of the business unit were strategically aligned and any hurdles in the lab, manufacturing, marketing or regulatory were quickly addressed leading to a very efficient program. This network also helped his own career. Besides two quick promotions, he had been tapped by the general manager of the business unit as the next director—the current director had hinted at retiring. The vocal support from his colleagues had made this an easy decision for the general manager. He was clearly on the fast track.

However, as with all good things, there was a sudden change in the market and the business unit was realigned. It resulted in the organization being split into two different business units. This manager still kept most of the people in the laboratory, but he was asked to serve other markets. His director was also changed. He went to work on understanding those markets and developing strategic plans for those markets with the new marketing organization while still continuing to support some of the products from his earlier role as they transitioned out of his scope of responsibilities. In addition, he found that his new boss was a micromanager with a very different style and different ideas than his. In all these changes, he forgot to rebuild his network. In a year, the new director reorganized her group and he was moved to an administrative position. He did not have his support group to pull for him. A year from then, there were major cuts in the business unit and he barely kept his job by moving to another division. Within a year, he had gone from the rising star to trying to keep his job.

His career was certainly impacted by changes made that were outside his control. Even if he had maintained a strong network, he might have still been badly affected. However, the network would have made him more effective that first year, making it more difficult for the new director to move him to a position of less influence. In addition, they would have pulled for him.

As you begin your career, you will find that for you to be successful in your programs, you will have to leverage resources, and influence decisions that are not part of your group or part of the functional team that is focused on a problem. Perhaps the only exception consists of assignments where you are asked to accomplish some work for a larger project that you can do by yourself. In fact, as you grow in your career, you will find that an increasing fraction of your job—and your success— depends on your ability to leverage resources and support outside your group or team. Your network refers to your connectivity with people who will be willing to make the extra effort to help you or bring in people they know to help you.

A proactive effort to grow your career also requires you to actively engage in network building. Look at your career strategy map and you will see that at any point in your career you will have to actively manage several potential opportunities or openings for your next job. You may look for openings because of layoffs, or you would like to advance but there are no openings in your organization, or you have to change jobs for other reasons. In each of these cases, you will have to know a group of people outside your current organization; more importantly, these people need to know and trust you enough to provide you with opportunities to grow in these other organizations outside your own.

When you begin your career in a company, your network is minimal. At best, you have a few friends you know from school or through past association who may be willing help you. Your primary support comes from your own group. Usually, when a group brings in a new person, they implicitly agree to support the person's efforts and are often willing to call on their own network to help this new person. Part of it is just the goodness of human nature, and part of it is that the success of the group also depends on the success of its members. In addition, they have probably hired you so that you can help them in some critical way—it behooves them to support you. From there on then, it is your responsibility to build your own network (and, of course, you will support new graduates joining your organization in future years).

Figure 2.5, for example, not only shows the people you work with but also shows how your network can evolve. Consider that you are working on a program as one of the core groups of people. You will need to connect with all other groups and understand what they are doing, provide input to their work based on how it affects the core program, and share what you are doing. If the core team (especially you) is focused on effective communications and a successful implementation, you will build a strong network of people in a variety of organizations and roles and at different points in their careers. Often, supervisors of people who are part of your network will visit to understand what the team is doing and the effectiveness of the program; this is an opportunity for you to make yourself known. (Beware of being too aggressive about self-promotion; it can ruin your reputation and the network you are building.) In addition, as you build your credibility, you might also work with the team leader to take responsibility of facilitating interactions with specific groups. This provides additional opportunities for you to get to meet supervisors of people who collaborate with you.

Figure 5.2 shows how your involvement in the program allows you to learn about people in other parts of the organization, learn about what they do, and learn about opportunities in those organizations. It also provides you with an opportunity to access leadership in those organizations as described. You could prioritize areas within this network based on your needs

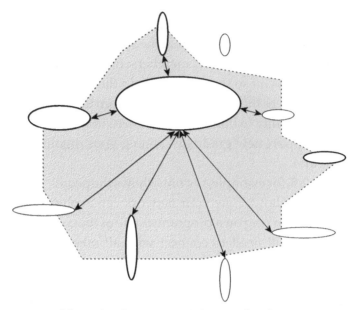

FIGURE 5.2. Schematic of your potential network, where you are a core member of a team.

for functional collaboration for your programs as well as organizations that might help you grow. The schematic in Figure 5.2 shows prioritized organizations by bold line (or dashed line) ovals. Are any of these organizations part of your career strategy map, and should you update your map based on your learnings from this collaboration?

In a supporting role, you may have to be more proactive to learn about other enabling groups or functions because you may not directly interact with all of the supporting teams. As in Figure 5.2, though, it is worthwhile thinking about which other organizations would help you be more effective in your work—even if you do not collaborate with them at this time. In addition, which groups might help you grow more. Prioritizing these can help you be more effective in building your network.

On the other hand, if you are not a member of the program's core team but work on specific portions of the program, you

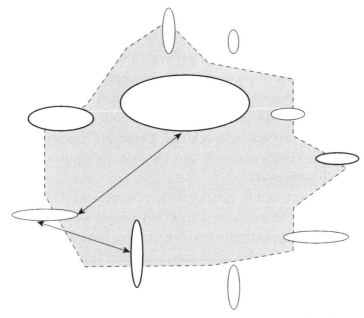

FIGURE 5.3. Schematic of your potential network as a result of a project where you support or enable the core team.

have an opportunity to collaborate with the core team as well as other people in the network of Figure 5.3 who interact with you. You begin to know them and they get to know you and understand how well you work, your leadership qualities, your creative abilities, and so on. In addition, you also have an opportunity for the managers and supervisors of the core team to know you. Figure 5.3 thus also provides you with an opportunity to expand your network, depending on your role within that network. And that is true for every project in which you participate. Your work ethic and your level of effective communications will determine how much of this group of people you engage and connect into your network.

Some part of building your network happens automatically, as described above. However, some part of building your network is also deliberate. In days of yore, the latter was not considered important; in fact, colleagues often looked down on individuals who were deliberate about "schmoozing." However, in today's environment of layoffs, it is important that your network is able to get you other jobs. This implies that you also know people outside your organization. Deliberate networking requires a significant effort—that is, energy and time. How do you optimally network and how much time do you spend networking? These are questions you have to answer for yourself. But the first question is how do you build networks?

As you start out in your company, some organizations set up a process where you get to meet key people with whom you may have the opportunity to work. If there is no such process, ask your group leader or manager to help introduce you to either people with similar skills or people with similar or related roles in the organization. This is an easy way to introduce yourself and get to meet people—your first step at network building.

A manager in an IT company (whose business model is built around providing IT solutions to companies that provide retail and healthcare services) told us that for employees to succeed in their company, strong networking skills were more important than technical skills. A large number of employees in this company form teams that are located on site with their client organizations. At these sites, the teams provide IT solutions to their clients—such as developing web-based software so that people can buy online from the site, or developing software so that online visitors can find the right solution for themselves using as few inputs as possible. In such a model, the key component of success is efficient and reliable service to the customer.

The manager pointed out that the company did not depend on all its technical employees being computer science experts or algorithm developers. The company only expected that these employees implement known algorithms and codes custom designed for the client's needs. The algorithms and codes are well known and can be learned quite easily. In such a situation, success of any employee depended on how well they interacted with the clients and provided them solutions for the problem. To do this, they needed to interface well with the client at the technical and social level. In addition, success also depended on how well they networked with other members of the IT organization, often located in different parts of the world; to ensure that the most efficient solutions were available to the customer and when specific custom requirements led to difficult implementation, they could quickly use the network to solve the problem.

The strength of the network helped employees in such organizations by:

- *Helping the employees developing and implementing solutions to unusual or custom problems*
- *Understanding the customer's real—and unarticulated—needs; also, understanding other needs that continue to come up for IT solutions and thus ensuring more business for the IT company*
- *Finding opportunities for personal growth*

The most natural, the easiest, and the necessary way to build your network is to do your job well. If you do not do your job well, irrespective of what else you do, you will have a shaky network. People may be nice to you and may be polite, but it is doubtful they will recommend you strongly enough or make an effort to help you when you may need it. And you have to be pleasant as you do your job—a teammate that people like working with, or at least someone that people do not dread on their teams. No one will make the effort to help an obnoxious teammate, and we have heard numerous examples of such people (with appropriate sighs and rolling of the eyes). As a new graduate, this avenue is your most important way to build a network. You are building your reputation as well. People do not know you. No one is dying to network with you. How you perform on the projects and teams is the most critical piece. And this is fortunate because building your network does not distract from your work.

As a new graduate, another way to build your network is to offer to help beyond the scope of your predefined responsibilities. If it takes a couple of hours or even a day, and as long as you do not spend 20% of your year working on such problems, offer to help people solve their problems when you can. They remember your help and when people are fighting deadlines and trying to meet program goals, your support will often be much appreciated and remembered. Having said this, do not walk around the company asking people how you can help them. As you get to know people in your group, or as you participate in programs with your team, ask people what they are working on, what are their projects. As they talk about it, share your interests, if any, so that they get to know your expertise. You may find that either you can develop something that helps them do their job better or more efficiently or you might be able to do a certain part of their job for them. Offer your help; and if the offer is taken up, make sure you deliver in a timely manner. It is not a problem not to offer to help—no one will will have a negative opinion of you. It is a problem if you offer to help and do not deliver or cause much delay. You will be the cause of their work being delayed.

Most organizations usually provide opportunities for "voluntary" work within their own organizations. These may include something as trivial as group picnics to something much more serious such as workshop sessions on certain technology domains or technical committees that may be relevant to the company. Other opportunities may include taking classes offered by the company, such as those on professional or personal development. Often these are cross-organizational activities bringing together people who may have limited opportunities to interact otherwise. Get to know what people are doing and what projects they work on and then either explore opportunities to collaborate or opportunities where you may be able to help them in some small way. If you find that these relationships are valuable, you might wish to connect with them at some regular frequency—maybe once every six months or so—by having lunch together or just meeting in an office space.

Conferences and professional collaborations are also good opportunities for building networks outside your company. The value of these networks cannot be understated in today's environment. When you have to leave this organization (which may be the result of numerous causes) and move to another, it is your network outside the organization that can help you. Conferences provide you with opportunities to meet with other professionals in various roles and fields from other organizations. They are often organized by professional associations that have numerous volunteering opportunities to help organize events at these conferences. These presentations, professional events, or opportunities to organize are all avenues to get to know people in other organizations, work with them in small projects or efforts that take little of your time, and get to know them and provide them with a way to know you.

You may also consider collaborating with faculty in universities and researchers in other labs when possible. Such collaborations help you continue to stay abreast with the technologies being developed, and they provide you with a chance to publish. In fact, whether it is through such collaborations or through those with your colleagues in your organization, publishing as regularly as possible is a good idea because publications (and presentations) keep people outside your organization in the know about the work you do and provide credible objective evidence about your competence. It helps when you wish to look for other jobs. Besides that, faculty and researchers in non-profit or government labs often interact with other industrial researchers as well—they can help connect you with others helping you with your network.

Having identified people who are important in your network, you also need to take the time to nurture those relationships—just like you would nurture a friendship. As in a friendship, make sure you have things that you share with these people. (However, unlike a friendship, keep this relationship professional unless both individuals clearly wish this relationship to develop into a friendship.) Otherwise, this process will be a drag to you and to the other person—you will not enjoy it at all and it will collapse. Build your relationships around what you share—whether it is interest in your respective kids or a hobby or a passion for science, or some area of your work. Make sure that what you share is dynamic; it cannot just be that both of you came from the same town, because then you will be done talking about that town in a couple of hours and be left with nothing. As in friendships, recognize that you are as interested in their well-being as you would like them to be interested in yours. Add aspects of your work and your careers onto those aspects of your life you share. Through your initial meetings, gain a clear understanding of how much you are willing and able to share and how much the other person is willing to share without either person becoming vulnerable or embarrassed. Through the first few meetings, it is important to have clear expectations; often it may be all right to be explicit about these expectations. These may include aspects of confidentiality or aspects that are to stay off limits in your conversations. It is also a good idea, if possible, to plan two or three different kinds of activities when you get together; for example, you might decide to meet over coffee sometimes and at other times have a game of tennis. This helps provide the relationship with opportunities of conversation as well as opportunities where you do not have to converse.

The description of networking seems to suggest that this can become a full-time job, and that is true. How do you find time to network while continuing to work on your programs, or how do you know when and where to network? Look at Figure 2.6 as it would map out for your current projects. Are there people who can help you work more effectively or who can provide support for the programs in which you participate today?

In addition, your career strategy map can also provide you with the key. Look at the map and locate where you are now (from Figure 5.4). If your career strategy map is up to date, you would have listed what your next possible jobs might be. Do you know at least three people who can provide you opportunities for each of the options you have listed as your next possible job (a checking question represented by the gray diamond in Figure 5.4)? In addition, also consider the jobs you

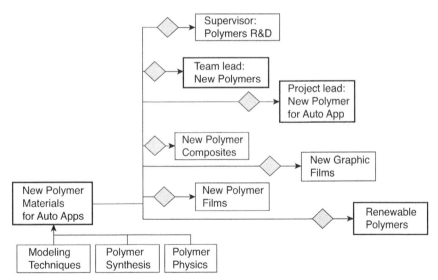

FIGURE 5.4. Schematic of your current position (and skills at this position) as well as your possible next position as a lateral move or as a position with more responsibility and leadership opportunity (irrespective of whether this is within your current company or outside). The gray diamonds are signs that ask you whether you have the resources (skills and network support) to access these positions. Rectangles with bold lines represent positions that you prefer.

identified as possible alternatives to this job—that is, opportunities for lateral moves. Similarly, can you identify three people who can help you access these positions? If these are too many, try and prioritize the opportunities you seek; this may help you network more optimally. As you do this, remember though that these networks are made up of humans. You will be significantly more successful if you see them as friends and colleagues and interact accordingly than if you see them just as resources who are there to help you.

With this in mind, you might also want to ask yourself about the effectiveness of your network. How effective is your network in helping you with your programs? When you need help, is your network able to point you to the right person or help you access the resources you need? Similarly, is your network in positions of leadership—can they get you information or help you access opportunities for growth when you are looking for them? Do they look out for you? You may even ask yourself if your network would be able to help you get to five interviews outside your organization and five inside your organization (you may choose other numbers, depending on your level of confidence) when you need them.

Networks are one of the most effective means of finding professional opportunities. One email from a mid-level manager in a Fortune 100 technology company describes the importance of networks as follows:

> "My first job after graduate school was a result of networking with someone who graduated a few years before I did and knew of my work. He forwarded my resume to a group looking for a specific expertise when the company itself was not hiring. The group invited me for an interview and I got the job. Subsequently, the opportunity I had to lead a project was a result of a manager who had seen my work in an earlier project. I had been in an enabling role for a project led by his group and obviously he liked my work ethics, results and my style of working with the team. He invited me to lead a project in his group—all other members of the team were from his group and I was the only individual from outside his group.

My opportunity to supervise was a result of my project leadership skills and after a few months of supervising a small group, when the director of the lab wanted to start a significant effort at developing a technology, he asked me to manage it even though I apparently did not have experience to manage such an effort. Since then, my effectiveness and leadership in managing a technology that had visibility with directors and senior management from around the company helped build my credibility as a manager. After a couple of years at this position, when I felt I was ready to move to a new challenge, a director who had an opening called me inviting me to interview for a position in his group. Again, the position was supposed to be beyond my level of experience; however, she had seen the last manager not be effective and was willing to try and my mentor told her about my experience. Since she knew of my work, she was willing to give me that opportunity; however, it was my mentor who planted that seed in her mind and convinced her that I might be a good candidate."

In fact, as one grows in ones career, moving higher up the ladder, recommendations play an important part of hiring people and hence networks play an increasingly important role in finding opportunities.

One last comment about networks—and we have placed this at the end of this discussion to highlight its importance. While your network will consist of numerous people in different positions within your organization's hierarchy (or in other organizations), find one set of people within your network who you can identify as your mentors. Make sure that you have mentors inside and outside the organization. Mentors are people with whom you build a special relationship, who understand your motivation, your expectations from your career, and goals in your career. They are people who understand you enough to critique aspects of your plans or their implementation, who guide your strategies and your long and short term goals. Often mentors are people in leadership positions or people with much experience in areas relevant to your career. They should be people who can help you understand and access information about opportunities and may be willing to help you access opportunities.

There is much that can be written about mentors[33]—books have been written on this subject. Within the context of networking, it is necessary to think about their role in your career. Mentors fulfill numerous roles. These include being a teacher, a guide, a counselor, a motivator, a sponsor, a coach, a role model, or one who helps open doors for you. Be clear about the role that a mentor should play (and they often play multiple roles but not all roles) when you set up your relationship. Choose mentors carefully based on your medium to long-term goals. You may also choose mentors who understand your background, your skills, and your motivations and can advise you to be successful with who you are. In addition, recognize that as times change, the dynamics of organizations and of the industry changes. Mentors who have had similar experiences decades ago may not be able to appropriately understand your situation or guide you if they do not understand how times have changed. Often people who are relevant to your career trajectory and are not in your direct hierarchy will be happy to mentor you—you need to ask them. Having said that, it is your job to nurture that relationship to make it meaningful.

While an individual may be willing to become your mentor, his continuing in that relationship depends on the value you bring to it. Often people mentor because they grow through advising or teaching. It also helps them find newer perspectives or outlook. If the mentor is someone within your own organization or industry, she may learn how people at your position are seeing things, what is and what is not working within the company or the industry. These are useful perspectives. What they are not looking at doing is listening to you complaints or being nagged about opportunities or sharing gossip. While this may be true for all relationships in your network, it is especially

---

[33]W. B. Johnson and C. R. Ridley, *The Elements of Mentoring*, Palgrave Macmillan, 2008.

true for mentoring relationships. In having a relationship with a person in a leadership position, ensure that when you have the need for advice with difficult situations, you also bring potential solutions to the table so that the mentor does not have to do all the thinking—it also shows your leadership abilities. Use the mentoring relationship to become a stronger leader. Most of all, do not ask for doors to be opened; show your strengths and abilities so that when a mentor hears that a colleague at his level has an opening, he is proud to introduce you as a possible candidate.

MANAGING YOURSELF

Numerous management gurus have argued that the ability to manage yourself can make your career and help you fulfill your potential or become a significant barrier to you achieving your goals. One component of managing yourself is discipline—the practice of implementing your strategies, due diligence at your work, and doing what you need to do despite a variety of distractions.

The other component is about managing yourself by understanding your strengths and weaknesses. It is important to understand "what I am good at and what do I not do very well, how I learn and how I operate, and how do I manage my time to stay focused and perform effectively." Numerous management gurus, including Peter Drucker,[34] argue that one should play to one's strengths. It takes much more work to take your area of weakness and make you average in that area. It is much easier for you to be an expert in an area of strength. Recognizing your strengths and weaknesses thus lets you plan your work such that you can focus and excel at your strengths while continuing to support your weaknesses through strong collaborations.

[34]P. Drucker, *Management Challenges for the 21ˢᵗ Century*, Harper Collins, 1999.

For example, you may be an expert in understanding technology landscapes, recognizing patterns in the directions taken by your competition, and thereby building your own technology strategies. However, you may be bad at people skills and in articulating. If that is the case, it perhaps makes most sense to you and to your organization that you spend your time on building the strategy while a collaborator helps to articulate the strategy and get buy in from key stakeholders or in inspiring a team to implement the strategy. Similarly, you might find that you are a very strong in organizational and emotional intelligence—your technical intelligence is perhaps average. In that case, your best strategy is to collaborate with someone who has technical vision.

The big question then is, Do you know your strengths and weaknesses? And if you do not, how do you learn about them? The most direct way is through feedback and self-analysis. Drucker points to simple self-analysis processes developed and practiced centuries ago by Ignatius of Loyola and John Calvin, independently. Individuals write down expected impact of key decisions or ventures and then over time track which aspects have gone per plan, where they have done better, and where they have not done well. This helps them recognize—over a period of a couple of years—their own strengths and weaknesses.

Another method, which perhaps requires less discipline but could lead you to understand your strengths and weaknesses, is the use of "360-degree feedback" tools that allow your peers, your immediate management, and people who report to you (if any) to assess your style, your strengths, and your weaknesses. While you may not agree with all of the analysis, it may point to you how people perceive you—breaking the perceptions by hierarchy. You thus get a sense of how people higher up perceive you and if that is different from the perception of peers or those who report to you. Does that imply you behave differently across the hierarchy—and, if so, why? This provokes you to self-analysis as well. If this method is used in combination of analysis of your performance in the past few years, then you can build a strong understanding of your strengths and weaknesses.

One senior manager described his fears as he started in his first managerial position. Would he be able to have frank and to-the-point discussions on performance with people who reported to him? How would he deal with conflicts? At the end of his first year, he received feedback that he had great people skills—that was a surprise. He would never have expected that trait in himself—at best, he said, he was sensitive to people's needs. That feedback, though, made him recognize how strong he was in that area. That gave him much more confidence dealing with people issues. His confidence in handling conflicts grew. Earlier he would beat around the bush, being tentative about pointing out to people in his group about their significant weaknesses or how certain aspects of their performance was affecting their work. The feedback helped him become more to the point while not losing touch with his sensitivity.

He found that, as a result, people were more engaged with him as a manager even when he presented them with negative reviews. They did not always agree with his assessment, but they recognized that he was trying to be fair and always advocated for them as appropriate. That helped people in his group engage with him as he attempted to make suggestions about performance, conflicts, and people strategies.

Recognizing his strength in people skills also helped him drive programs for effectively. He always knew that he was technically strong and was talented in developing technical strategies. An understanding of his strengths in people skills gave him more confidence in putting together teams to implement these strategies. He took greater initiative in planning and driving programs to help the company grow, knowing that people respected how he treated them and thus he continued to become better in how he was able to motivate and collaborate with people.

Drucker warns that individuals who are extremely good in one area often assume that other skills are irrelevant or worthless. Thus, scientists and technologists often think little of human resource experts or of accountants, and business experts think less of technologists. In thinking of other skills as insignificant, one usually ignores building collaborations with those skilled in areas of one's own weakness, and that can have only limited effectiveness and lead to the failure of an effort.

A caveat, perhaps. Even though the premise of this discussion is that one should play to one's strengths and not worry about one's weakness, the reality of organizational functions suggests that this is not completely true. Depending on the organization, its culture, and one's functions, one might have to develop one's skills in areas of weakness to meet some minimal standards. For example, irrespective of your function and the organization, you will need to have some minimal level of social intelligence. Misbehaving with people will not be accepted; and irrespective of your technical genius, if you are rude or verbally abusive with people, your career will be severely affected, and you may also get fired.

It is also important to think about how we spend out time at work. As you grow into your job, you will often find numerous requests for help on a number of fronts. Some of these may be from colleagues who want you to give them some input on their projects. Others only want to use you as a sounding board. Yet others perhaps request an afternoon's worth of help from you. In addition, there are a number of administrative needs that your group would like done, and it is often shared among all members of the group. Mandatory courses, as well as forms to be filled, all take time. There are also calls to volunteer for various community and team building efforts within any organization. In addition, there is email. And you have not even begun to think about your projects. In managing your career, you also have to manage how you spend your time. One tool that has been recommended in various forms is a time-accounting tool.

Study how you spend your time over the next month (you can decide the level of detail). Record how much time you spend on emails, on your projects, on interacting with people in the hallway, on helping people by listening to their programs and giving them advice, on spending an afternoon helping someone with their project (one with which you are not formally connected), on voluntary efforts in team building, and so on. Next to each category, also record key gains from the time spent. For example, perhaps you learned about an algorithm that might be useful by listening to your colleagues program. Or the person down the hall told you about an opportunity for collaboration as you were chatting with her. Or you met someone who you would love to have as your mentor through a volunteer program.

Now ask yourself how these successes are of value to your career. Whether directly or indirectly, how much do they help you grow? Only you can rate yourself on this. For some people, the growth that comes through community building within the organization is significant. For others, nothing compares to discovering a new structure or inventing a new algorithm; meetings and social niceties are mere irritants that can be ignored.

Perhaps you could use a scale of 1 to 5 (or any other of your choice) to highlight for yourself which of your efforts give you most satisfaction and help you grow.

Once you have done this, analyze what you see. Do you spend too much time taking care of paperwork—work that needs to be done but does not give you any satisfaction? Do you spend too much time chatting in the hallways or helping others? On the other hand, does your analysis show that you do no networking at all? This analysis begins to point to areas of your work schedule that need attention. They point to changes you perhaps need to make in a disciplined manner— whether you make them or not is a different discussion.

They also provoke thought about whether you are avoiding certain activities. Are you avoiding networking because you do not enjoy it? You might decide that you do not care about it—but let that be a conscious discussion (based on a realization of what you gain or lose through this activity), not a result of an underlying discomfort you may have of making "small talk" that could be addressed with some coaching. Similarly, are you avoiding working on a certain project because you do not like certain people on the team? These are questions that can help you find strategies to solve a problem that you may be avoiding or one which you have not recognized.

Often, when we move from one job to another, we continue to keep a number of practices that we had developed that were appropriate in the first job. With changes in jobs or in the nature of the same job, responsibilities change. Thus, how we are appraised also changes. It would be naive, then, to assume that the practices that were effective in one set of responsibilities would also be effective later. This requires that we review how we spend our time and how we can be effective. During such transitions, it is important to analyze our time and schedule with some variant of time-accounting tool.

For example, perhaps you have moved from being the product developer in unit A to the product developer in unit B that meets the needs of a different market. In market A, perhaps the technology was fast-moving. New inventions were being made everyday. It was expected that you would spend a significant amount of time looking at technical publications so that you would know who was doing what and how that affected your organization's strategies. Is market B similar? If the technology is slower-moving, do you need to spend as much effort scanning journals? Does the need in such an area change from constantly understanding the technology changes to understanding consumer needs perhaps? Or perhaps more time spent in developing prototypes?

The same is also true when the nature of the job changes; for example, perhaps you were working on one project for an external customer while now you work on three projects for internal customers. The time you spent in putting together reports that were of publication quality may have been appropriate and effective for the external customer—are they necessary now? Time spent attending to every complaint of the external customer was critical to helping your organization profit. Do you need to be ready to jump every time an internal customer calls, or can that feedback be addressed in weekly meetings?

Management experts even suggest that this is a tool that one should use once every year, perhaps. Over time, we change how we do things. Habits creep in. A tool such as this provides a conscious check so that we can revise our working style and keep high levels of effectiveness. This tool is not a magic wand that helps you be more effective; all it does is help you become more conscious about how you are spending your time and whether you are being disciplined about your work plan.

SUMMARY

Your career and its growth is based on consistent and continuous evidence that you can scope and solve problems of increasing complexity. As a technical expert starting out, establishment of your technical expertise is expected and is the best place to begin, and it can be achieved most easily if you plan your programs and manage your expectations well. However, broader skills are necessary for success—skills that require you to (a) intelligently survey the organization and gather information that can help you make strategic decisions, (b) facilitate and

leverage interaction with other experts to solve problems, and
(c) implement solutions and then package and deliver these
solutions as appropriate. An effective network helps you access
and effectively leverage the organization, while success with
your programs rests on strong communication and collaboration skills.

As a new employee, you are not expected to be expert at these.
However, you are expected to learn these skills. As you use these
skills and learn various methods for collaborating, communicating, and building your network, you continue to grow and
make a case for yourself for bigger and better opportunities.

KEY TAKEAWAYS

1. Having been hired into a technical position, your first
   goal is to establish your technical credentials—that is,
   that you are a person who understands the technical
   details of a problem and is willing to go into those
   details to truly grasp what is happening and that your
   decisions are based on such a process. You become a
   person who is wanted on various teams because people
   know that you can solve problems.

2. Maintain a portfolio of programs to manage your probability of success. If you are working on long-term programs, ensure that you have short- and mid-term goals
   built into the program—goals that would be aligned to
   company strategies and would by themselves solve some
   key problem or provide opportunity for growth. If you
   are working on short-term programs, ask what else these
   programs could empower across the company.

3. Aim to establish yourself as an expert in at least
   one area. Understand the markets that are affected by

technologies in this area, and study key players interested in these technologies. Be aware of all technology development in this area (ongoing and historical) as well as their commercial implications (for your company). Also learn about technology areas that overlap with or are conjugate to this area of expertise, at least with respect to your company's strategy.

4. Good communication empowers effective flow of information and analysis in a large and complex network such as a large company, thus ensuring that critical decisions are made and implemented. Recognize your own strengths and weaknesses in communication processes, recognize that multiple paths of communication are possible, and choose appropriate methods of communication to be effective. Share important information and analysis to key stakeholders in your projects to ensure that critical decisions are being taken vis-à-vis your program. Also be certain that you have access to information about higher-level strategies and trends to ensure that your plans are consistent with these high-level strategies.

5. In collaborating with people, recognize the different motivations that drive them and build your strategy based on these different needs. Collaboration is a process of shared evolution and implementation of ideas; good communication allows you to build and sustain that shared space. Understand the dynamics of the teams in which you participate. Do the members believe in themselves, is there an environment of intellectual equality, is this a team of leaders, and is there a safe space where members can be candid and critical without any repercussions? While these are the ideal conditions, recognizing

how your team fares with respect to these characteristics will help you focus on how you can overcome
its shortcomings—usually through effective
communication.

6. Understand the culture—the unwritten laws—of the
   team. How and when is information shared with stakeholders and who shares it? How are initiatives taken
   and implemented? How are decisions made? Work
   with them to the extent that you can and understand
   how you can work around them when you need to. You
   can do this only on the strength of strong personal
   relationships and effective communication.

7. To be successful in your programs, you will have to
   leverage resources and will need to influence decisions
   that are not part of your group or part of the functional
   team that is focused on a problem. What key skills or
   information would critically help your project and how
   can you access them? Who are key people among your
   current co-workers who complement your skills, or
   who could help you connect with problems and opportunities that interest you?

8. Be proactive in building your network. Stay connected
   with members of past teams—those with whom you
   collaborated or those who you helped on projects.
   Your network should include those who can help
   you be more effective in your work or who can help
   you be more useful to your company by engaging
   in more challenging problems at higher levels of
   responsibility.

9. Mentors form a key component in planning your
   career. In the long term, they should be able to
   provide insight into forces that will affect your career
   choices. In the short term, they should be familiar

with the kinds of problems and challenges you face and be an advisor to help you navigate these within the cultural framework of your company. In addition, they should have the network to provide you insight into opportunities or help you build your network to solve your problems. Choosing and building the right mentoring relationships can be critical in helping you build your career.

10. Recognize that you will have multiple tasks that you will have to accomplish on a regular basis—administrative, strategic, project related, voluntary activities, and so on. Ensure that you prioritize based on your goals and how they affect your short-term and long-term performance evaluation. Evaluate which ones play to your strengths and which ones help you add skills. Also evaluate whether your routine includes tasks that are no more relevant or should be delegated to others. Identify efforts that are most aligned to your strategy and ensure that they are well-implemented.

LEADERSHIP AND GROWTH

As you establish yourself, and people around recognize that you are right for the job and that your solutions work, they begin to trust you and value what you bring to the table. In the "good old days," this was the sufficient and necessary condition for management to consider you for more responsibility and promotion. Today, however, management expects you to be performing at the next level,[35] taking on more challenging problems and greater responsibilities before you are considered for promotion. So how do you go about doing that (without stepping on other toes)? How do you show the organization that you can do well at a higher position without being at that position? In today's work environment, such leadership is recognized as helping the organization grow beyond what you have been chartered to do and is necessary for you to grow.

As you start as a new employee, you are perhaps overwhelmed with numerous terms, processes, groups, departments, and divisions in the company and are trying to make sense of your current job needs through all of this. Yet, you are

---

[35]Some companies will explicitly state that you should be performing at the next level for you to be considered for promotion. In others, this is implicit.

Planning a Scientific Career in Industry: Strategies for Graduates and Academics
By Sanat Mohanty and Ranjana Ghosh
Copyright © 2010 John Wiley & Sons, Inc.

already a leader—the company hired you to lead a certain area and take on a certain responsibility. You will thus be expected to show technical leadership in this area soon—even as a new employee. This book has already provided the framework to help you understand your job and how it connects with the goals and strategies of your company. As you gain expertise on the functional aspects of your job, you will be expected to show leadership in aligning with the company goals as part of your function and subsequently leveraging that function for greater profits through efficiency or growth. While leadership and your next position may seem like longer-term goals now, we would suggest that you begin to understand what it means and that you also learn processes, practices, and tools and put them to practice in your work right away.

In this chapter we will focus on leadership within the industrial context and how it helps you grow. We discuss what leadership in the industry means—especially from the perspective of a knowledge worker—and try to identify skills and experiences that would help a new employee. We will discuss what it means to be a leader, styles of leadership and skills you must consciously build or hone, and how you manage yourself so you are effective in growing and being a leader. Any growth in today's industrial context is based on leadership, broadly defined. Your growth (taking on additional responsibility in technical, business, or strategy management functions) depends on your ability to lead, by providing solutions and skills that coach and convince a team or an organization down a path and help to deliver results. There is no other path for effective and sustainable growth.

LEADERSHIP OF TEAMS

Leadership is rather loosely used, and it is appropriate that we spend some time talking about leadership and what it means. To "lead" is a verb with the following meanings: to go before or with to show the way; to conduct or escort: to lead a group on a cross-country hike; to conduct by holding or guiding; to influence or induce; to guide in direction, course, action, opinion, and so on; to command or direct (an army or other large organization); to be superior to; have the advantage over; to have top position or first place in. It is instructive that we generally think of a leader as one who commands or directs based on an authority invested through hierarchy. In fact there are many connotations of "lead" and many ways to lead.

Defining leadership is a popular topic with numerous industrial and management journals. One[36] typical article carries enumerates qualities of good leaders. Citing business guru Peter Drucker, it says that effective leaders have the following traits: Integrity and honesty; loyalty; optimism and courage; selflessness; knowledge; and competency in the industry; ability to make the most with available talent; and dependability. It is significant that nowhere in the characterization of a leader does it lay claim to authority or power.

While this note in a popular magazine points to key characteristics of leaders, these characteristics do not make them leaders. There are numerous low- and mid-level managers with these traits who are not leaders. In addition, there are numerous leaders who are very successful but do not have all of these characteristics. It is difficult to define leadership only on the basis of manifested characteristics—something that most popular magazines are wont to highlight. Numerous researchers studying leadership in the industry and in society today argue that leadership is as much a result of processes used by individuals, how they think about problems and opportunities, their self-management, and their intelligences as it is about such manifested characteristics.

[36]http://www.nfib.com/object/IO_20132.html; http://ezinearticles.com/? Business—7-Characteristics-Of-Leaders-&id=395903; http://www.power-homebiz.com/vol53/traits.htm;

The general consensus is often of a leader as an authoritative figure driving a group or an organization on the basis of power. Unfortunately, that rarely works in the industry in today's circumstances, especially for knowledge workers. While the media can glamorize General Patton effectively ordering his troops and inspiring them by loud rhetoric or present football coaches shouting invectives at their players and insulting them to get them to play harder, imagine what would happen if your boss tried that in your work area. Invariably such a boss would lose her group's respect as well as their willingness to engage with her. Even though she may be able to get them to do certain things on the basis of her authority (annual appraisals, pay raises, promotions, etc.), she will not be able to get them to engage with her on major problems or situations where they need to stretch their creative abilities and inventive skills.

Given changes in the industry, it is perhaps not pragmatic to be a "bossy" supervisor—increasingly, one learns about instances where an individual may have his former "boss" reporting to him. In addition, unlike in the military or in a job that requires physical performance, the environment of a knowledge worker does not make it conducive to lead through aggression or fear. A knowledge worker produces value for a company through analysis of situations, invention, and application of solutions—all mental processes that cannot be coerced by force or power. Thus, leadership driven primarily by power is set up to fail.

There are times when a boss needs to be assertive, in holding individuals or a team accountable or preventing inappropriate behavior or even in leading a team in a particular direction. However, if that is the only style of leadership you can access, then you are in for a difficult career. An effective boss needs multiple leadership tools and styles for different situations. For the most part, even a boss with his "power" can work most effectively through being accountable to the group as much as he expects them to be accountable and by engaging his team on problems of strategic importance. The boss's leadership is in making the case for the importance of a problem or the direction or strategy of the group or of a solution. Leadership is in active buy-in so that the team can engage. Once members of the team are engaged, they will drive themselves; most individuals would know the importance of their work and recognize what is at stake if they succeed or fail. Knowledge workers are passionate about their work and love the intellectual component; they do not require a slave driver to achieve results. Leadership at that point requires ensuring a positive environment, guiding direction and pointing opportunities, facilitating open discussions and collaboration, effective interaction, and disciplined progress so that the team stays on track. None of these requires an aggressive form of leadership modeled after ultra-aggressive football coaches or military sergeants that the media likes to glamorize.

In fact, the dynamics described above empowers leadership without hierarchical power. In the technology industry, bosses are not the only leaders. Each knowledge worker is extending the field (within the organization or globally) in unique ways and is a leader in his or her right. In addition, the knowledge worker also needs to ensure that this new knowledge learned is relevant and applied to a larger team or broader goals; this also requires leadership. Without access to power to lead, she must lead through other means. An aggressive model of leadership will fail. One's leadership style needs to be driven by facilitation and communication based on knowledge, analysis, and one's own credibility. Fortunately, this style of leadership can help you influence all aspects of leading teams that are focused on understanding scenarios and developing solutions. Increasingly, industries are beginning to trust and value such leadership more than the archetypal power driven boss.

This model of teams of leaders—and of working styles—is much more empowering than the traditional power-based one. In the latter, the boss is the only leader and everyone jockeys to get his position or to win favors with him. The former is empowering because of its potential to build a team of leaders, not just a leader with his team. Most teams are built to tackle a problem whose resolution requires a wide variety of expertise and skill sets. One single leader has neither the ability nor the bandwidth to understand or explore all options within each of these areas. The team needs leaders who can truly explore each of those areas and lead through inventions or creative solutions as well as understand the interdisciplinary implications of these solutions. In addition, members of the team also need to lead in other areas that affect the whole team—for example, understanding markets, business alignment, intellectual property management, time/resource management, and so on. *An effective team is truly a team of leaders.*

PROMISE-BASED LEADERSHIP

Studies show that individuals are more willing to respect promises or commitments that they made voluntarily based on their own engagement with the problem. Individuals who have committed to such goals are often willing to stretch themselves to meet those commitments; and delays, when they occur, are owing to real hurdles and challenges and not mere excuses. Such commitments need to have the following characteristics:

1. These are publicly made so they cannot be conveniently forgotten by those who made them. Similarly, those who required the commitment cannot renege from their own responsibilities once it is fulfilled. This may be driven by an individual perception of being honorable and

recognizing that commitment made to peers or to a team—and its success or failure—affects the team.

2. These are made through active engagement, collaboration, and negotiation by all involved. All parties then can take ownership of the commitment and its implications. They are not requests defined by one party and then thrown over organizational fences for another group to address.

3. These are voluntarily made. Studies show that when individuals feel coerced into a commitment or feel that the commitment was distorted, they will only make a partial effort to fulfill it and may only fulfill it partially based on what they feel is justified.

4. These are explicit—with details such as who will do what, under what conditions, what deadline, who will then take it over, and so on. There is no room for confusion, and all parties are accountable to each other. Explicitly defined commitments ensure execution across the various stakeholders, without anyone left feeling cheated. While such explicit commitments allow for renegotiation based on dynamic circumstances, they also provide a well-defined state from which to negotiate.

5. These are well-grounded in the broader strategy of the organization. Everyone clearly understands why they are doing what they are doing, and they can take ownership of the motivation for the commitment. This helps people appreciate that they are not committing themselves to useless tasks.

Sull and Spinosa's proposal[37] of promise-based leadership is built on the idea that societies are built on social interactions;

[37]D. N. Sull and C. Spinosa, Promise based management: The essence of execution, *Harvard Business Review*, April 2007.

and while written contracts are important today, social inter-actions are based on the value of what people say to each other. An individual's reputation among her peers is depen-dent on whether an individual reports truthfully as well as whether the individual is a woman of her words. This peer influence is usually successful in motivating individuals to follow up on their commitments. Promise-based management attempts to take advantage of this, driving commitment through verbal contracts between groups or individuals rather than through usual carrot-and-stick programs of promotion and appraisals.

It is effective in the new world of industrial organizations with matrix management structures where you cannot influ-ence just through hierarchy or position. In addition, this is also significant because it empowers everybody—not just those with positional power—to influence action and deci-sions. As a new employee, understanding and becoming good at promise-based leadership has great potential. It allows you to (a) develop relationships and request help from in-dividuals who are more experienced than you and (b) access support from other organizations effectively without having to need the leverage of hierarchy. This can become a tool to help you operate successfully and develop your leadership abilities in developing your programs and helping your organization grow.

Studies such as this strongly suggest that effective leader-ship of knowledge workers is based on engagement and discussion rather than command and direction, even when leadership can access hierarchical power. *Effective leadership is driven by early understanding of a situation based on extensive research and recognition of patterns, identification of strategies based on scenario planning and analysis, and the ability to engage with a team and facilitate a team consensus around both in a way that the team owns the problem, the strategies, the solutions and its implementation*. If leadership is not *de facto* based on position of power, it opens up opportunities for leadership to all who are able and willing—not just to the boss or the manager. Recognizing this and acting on it can provide significant opportunities for growth; it depends critically, though, on managing ones self actively.

As an individual without positional power, leadership requires you to help yourself and the team recognize the larger context within which your work is relevant (timelines, market changes, competitive trends and plans, etc.). It implies that you use this understanding to provide options as well as discipline to the team: Should the team look at other technologies? Should it change its timeline? Is the program within budget? Are critical projects within the program progressing? This does not require power or hierarchy either; it requires that all members of the team have bought into the need for this program, recognize its context, and are working to meet well-defined goals. It does require effective communication, strong collaborative practices, and an effective network—all aspects that we have discussed in the earlier chapter on establishing yourself. Leadership is thus your ability to use these technical and people skills to help the team move in a direction that is consistent with larger strategic goals.

Even as a new employee, then, promise-based leadership provides you with some tools that you can use to get help from your colleagues to develop or implement a new idea or work on a problem that is important but has not been staffed. Business and technical discussions with these colleagues can help clearly scope the problem and your approach as well as identify key stakeholders and milestones. Detailed plans and commitment to well-defined actions as described above could be used to get a program going. You could be showing leadership with a new idea or program despite having no hierarchical power—that would be evidence of leadership.

LEADERSHIP AND TECHNICAL ACUMEN

In industries that are based on developing and providing technology-based products or services (as opposed to retail or transportation or entertainment, for example), a leader must have strong technical acumen. Technical acumen refers to a sound understanding of the fundamentals of the science and technologies that are core to the industry. Thus, a leader in a company focusing on building communication networks must have a strong understanding of the fundamentals of network theory. A leader in a company that develops metal composites must have a strong understanding of the science of metals. In addition, the leader must also have an up-to-date sense of trends in the industry. While he or she may not be the expert in each of the areas that are being pioneered within the field, the leader must know about these pioneering efforts and recognize the impact of these efforts in the field. For example, the leadership in Microsoft understands the impact of Linux and has taken proactive steps to address the competition that arises from improving Linux systems. In doing this, it was not necessary for the CEO to be an expert on Linux.

For industries that use a business model based on technical innovation, such technical understanding is critical. A technical leader is a key driver of new technologies that can potentially change the business paradigm and the competitive landscape. A business leader is not expected to be the technical expert driving research and development; however, she is expected to recognize the larger picture of where technologies are headed and how they could influence the development of products, thus providing opportunities for significant growth. The business leader in a technology company is expected to point out development in specific areas or recognize the impact of R&D in these areas as they become relevant. There have been numerous cases of new technologies that developed and resulted in the collapse of giant corporations that were wedded to old technologies and could not maneuver to compete effectively with new technologies.[38] Examples include CDC (Control Data Corporation) and CRAY.

CDC and later Cray have both become quite irrelevant to the computing world though both were once giants. Both did not see the trajectory of technologies developing and were not able to deal with the impact of those technologies. CDC is now dead—though a few of the companies that spun off are quite successful. An example of Cray's inability to see the trajectory of computing technology was a comment by its CTO, who said that Linux was irrelevant to high-performance computing.

Another example is that of mobile phones. Companies that were unable to see the changing landscape of communication with the development of new technologies have been largely destroyed or severely affected. An example is Bell Company. At one point it was so powerful that it was forced to break up into small companies (the baby Bells) by the courts in the United States. Today, when one thinks of communication companies, the names that initially come to mind are Nokia, Ericsson, T-Mobile, and Sprint.

A third example includes numerous companies in the business of photofilms. Consider Fuji or Eastman Kodak. Both were giants in the business of making photographic films and cameras. Look at old movies; they were invariably shot on one of these two films. They were blind-sided by the coming digital technology; they did not embrace the technology since they felt that would affect their core technologies and businesses. Now people hardly use film-based cameras. When one thinks of cameras, one rarely considers Fuji; market leaders are include Canon, Sony, and Olympus. Kodak has done better.

[38]C. M. Christensen, *The Innovator's Dillema*, Collins Business, 2003.

Even for companies whose business model is not based on constant technology innovation, it is important to keep an eye on all technologies that might be relevant to the industry— technologies that might affect them, technologies that they could use to do better, or ones that could wipe them out. Consider the internet, for example. At one time, *Encyclopaedia Britannica* was a gold standard in encyclopedias. They were highly priced and were owned by very few people; they were very useful if you wanted to quickly learn about a wide set of subjects. They were also a status symbol. With the coming of the internet and with various software companies providing encyclopedias for free, it is very easy to find everything you want to know something about. In addition, with the dynamic ability of search engines as well as "wiki" tools that can be updated real time and have the latest knowledge about anything, *Encyclopaedia Britannica* became irrelevant. The company did not see this coming and were unable to deal with it.

The internet has also affected numerous industries. Retail stores—for example, Walmart and Amazon—that were able to leverage the impact of the internet have catapulted themselves into strong position compared with their competition. In fact, Walmart was able to leverage its efficient supply chain as well as the ability of databases and the internet to even take dominant position not only with respect to competition but also over manufacturers that provide it with goods to stock on its shelves. That was an unexpected change in dynamics in the supply chain based on the ability to understand and take advantage of technology.

There are leaders in the industry who have done well without deeply understanding technologies; however, they still have had strong technical acumen in understanding the direction of technologies, what could be done with them, and how one should manage them. Often, they surround themselves with leaders who understand the core technologies that affect the business, their trajectories, and the implications of developments in these technologies for the business. An example is 3M's McKnight, who himself began his career as a bookkeeper, but understood the significance of technology to the extent that he defined 3M's business model on technology innovation.

As a new employee, one who has recently graduated from school, you will have an in-depth understanding of the technologies that you have worked on. However, you may not have a lot of technical acumen because it is unlikely that you would have considered these technologies from an industrial perspective. You may not have mapped the competition, the use of their technologies, and how their technology choices are aligned with their business strategies. (Technologies can only be successful within the context of a company's strategy; open source models may not be an appropriate choice for a company such as Microsoft whose current revenue model is based on pricing of software.) It is also important to understand how their technology choices relate to their core technologies. For example, a petrochemical company will find it difficult to develop chemicals based on ethanol, without making some critical changes in its business models. Or a company that produces a certain chemical as a by-product will naturally choose a technology based on that by-product rather than choosing a competing technology.

In addition to understanding the fundamentals of a technology, technical acumen also involves an increased understanding of the trajectory of a technology and the context of the business. You would need technical acumen to answer questions such as which of the many R&D efforts driven by labs and universities truly affect the industry and which ones are interesting but not relevant. And when they are relevant, will they be useful 3 years from now or 10 years from now? You would need technical acumen to build a portfolio of technology or product development programs such that they include long- and short-term results and product across a timespan, because if one *only* bets on a technology that will deliver results 10 years later, by then the company might be decimated by competition that gained advantages by betting on a technology that bore fruit in only 3 years.

In essence, technical acumen is your ability to understand relevant technologies with respect to (a) the markets of interest to you, (b) how competition and competitive technologies affects the marketplace and your role in the marketplace, and (c) how you can manage these changes. You would then develop business strategy maps for your company based on its strengths and weaknesses while also understanding your competitions' strategy.

While you may not already have the technical acumen, you would have had the opportunity to develop various aspects of it, in the process of establishing yourself. With respect to a specific technology, you will have recognized all competitive technologies as well as variations and future developments. Literature and patent review would give you insight into critical questions being addressed and how each of them will affect you. You would have learned about your company's core and its business model as well the trajectory of choices it made in developing itself. Over time, you will begin to also learn more details about adjacent technologies. Thus, you have already begun to build your technical acumen and become increasingly ready to make choices and lead based on this knowledge.

LEAD A TEAM TO.... WHERE?

Where are the leaders planning to lead? In what direction and to what extent? Researchers have found that different individuals are good at different aspects of leadership. Some individuals are very good at building the vision and getting an organization successfully up and running. But they might fail in helping the organization grow further. Others who are very good at stream-lining operations and consolidating gains fail at helping start-ups. An example from outside the industrial realm presents Schumacher, the visionary who articulated "small is beau-tiful."[39] While he presented numerous examples of how this vision could be practically translated into small businesses or ventures to help sustainable economic efforts, it was up to his lieutenants, less visionary but much more detail-oriented, to lead the development of such efforts on the ground.

There are numerous examples of CEOs who have been outstanding in helping get start-up ventures established but have not been as successful growing the business. The same is also visible among mid-level management leaders as well as technical leaders. You will find technical leaders who are visionaries in scoping a new area of science and technology. They are brilliant in coming up with ideas and being energized in proving concepts and technical feasibility. Such leaders are very critical to a company: They can lead the organization to making major discoveries and inventions as well as in articu-lating the potential impact of new ideas. However, they quickly get bored of the tedious, repetitive experiments needed to fine-tune the technology while also engineering it for specific applications. They have mentally moved on to the next major challenge.

On the other hand, there are leaders who are more focused in studying the details of a problem. They are the individuals who will understand exactly which parameters might prevent a potential invention from becoming a commercial product and identify how the parameters of an invention can be designed so that it is feasible for scale-up, is robust to the variances of manufacturing, and can strategize details of these operations.

---

[39]E. F. Schumacher, *Small Is Beautiful*, Harper Perennial, 1989.

Or they may be the ones who set up the supply chain or the policies for customer interactions that allow us better market access. Whenever there is a problem, they will dig deep into the fundamentals, determine exactly what is amiss, and redesign the product or strategy so that it succeeds. They are happy to do repetitive studies, playing detective to identify the exact design window. While the business and scientific community often highlights the work of the dreamers and radical thinkers, these leaders are the backbone that deliver the successes of an organization.

A company needs both kinds of leaders. In certain times—especially in difficult economic times or in times when the market is consolidating—the organization needs managers who can drive discipline, focus on the details, and be efficient about these aspects (and yet be innovative about taking advantage of market opportunities). At other times—for example, when the economic environment allows for major opportunities—it is important that the organization be able to drive visionary growth (and yet be disciplined about implementation of that vision).

Organizational gurus point out that different kinds of situations require different kinds of leadership. There may be cases where:

1. The team needs leadership to reinforce strategies or policies. For example, central leadership may have decided that growth should be driven through improving efficiency and cutting costs. The team might need leadership in helping it acknowledge this strategy, reaffirm its importance, and focus on those goals. In other cases, it might need replication of best practices learned from across the company to be implemented within the team.

2. The team may have drifted from its core goals, and leadership may be needed in bringing the team back

into alignment. For example, perhaps in a certain economic environment, central leadership has strategized that the best path is to improve efficiency and consolidate in the market place. The team may have drifted into excessive diversification—for a variety of reasons—and might need leadership to get back with the plan.

3. The team might be going in the right direction, and the goal of the leader might be to push it further along through some incremental changes—by extending speed of development or stretch the goals of the team. For example, the team might be aiming for growth through adjacent markets. The leader's role might be to further strengthen that growth through more discipline or better implementation of tactics. Alternatively, the leader might help the team to extend the scope of application of the strategy to reach more adjacent markets.

4. The team might be going in the right direction but might be going too slowly. The goal of the leader might be to significantly accelerate development or extend goals. For example, the leadership might challenge the team to analyze even more far-out markets that might be riskier but have higher returns. Or it might challenge the team to restrategize growth in adjacent markets to achieve that growth faster.

5. Leadership might be required to change the direction of the team. For example, perhaps changes in the market or the global environment requires the team to refocus and gain position in the value chain within the core rather than diversifying into adjacent markets. Or the team might be required to focus on a completely different market or a new technology strategy based on specific feedback.

6. A team might realize that it has gone in a direction that is unfeasible or counterproductive and needs to start over. For example, the team may have completely misunderstood the needs of the market and developed a technology with such an incorrect understanding. Leadership would require that the team get back to the drawing board and start fresh.

In reality, teams have to make decisions on how they focus on technical growth, growth in collaborative processes, and marketing strategies, among others. Thus leadership might choose to have one kind of leadership focus on technical growth (perhaps inspiring for accelerated growth) while focusing on a different kind of growth in collaborative practices (perhaps choosing to reinforce industry best practices within the team) and a third in marketing strategies (perhaps choosing to realign with core strategy). The leadership of the team must recognize this multidimensional focus and address the details of implementing its strategies in all these dimensions. Gains made in technical innovation, for example, may slip if leadership also does not keep focus on implementation of collaborative processes for example.

As a new employee, your job is to recognize scenarios that provide opportunities for leadership and learn leadership tools as they apply in these situations. Consider the direction of your teams. What is the current position and direction of these teams, and how do they progress? Given that your initial strength and experiences lie in the technical domain, it would be appropriate and natural for you to be involved in this domain. It would be useful to ask where the team should go and what its strategy should be. How are other entities (companies, labs) with expertise in this area progressing? What progress has your team made in IP, prototype or product development, market understanding, and business development, and where are they lacking? Outside the domain of the technology, per se, it would be useful for you to learn decision-making processes that the team currently uses. How does it map its IP plans or market presence? How does it review its project and manage its program? Are these processes the same for different kinds of programs (for example, ones that need to move quickly versus ones that need a portfolio of products and are thus slow)? As part of the team, you might be able to participate in planning and implementing these aspects of your project. Through this process, you gain an understanding of trajectory and management of projects or programs as used, along with an understanding of their strengths and opportunities for improvement.

LEADERSHIP AND MULTIPLE INTELLIGENCES

In the last decade, numerous cognitive scientists have presented data and formulated theories to strongly suggest that humans actually have "multiple intelligences"[40] that are distinct from each other physiologically and psychologically. Industrial behavior experts and management gurus have also come to believe that multiple intelligences are relevant to leadership as well. These scientists argue (based on experimental studies, greater physiological understanding of the brain, and correlations in case studies) that our cognitive processes in each of these forms of intelligences evolve almost independently (thus a musical prodigy may have a normal cognitive development in math skills or a mathematical genius may have little linguistic skills) but depend quite strongly on both innate talents and the environment and experiences.

---

[40]One set of multiple intelligences proposed by Howard Gardner (*Frames of Mind: The Theory of Multiple Intelligences*, Basic Books Inc., 1983) includes linguistic intelligence, logical–mathematical, spatial, bodily–kinesthetic, musical, interpersonal, intrapersonal, and naturalist.

This means that even though you may be intelligent in technical matters (owing to latent talent and years of training), it does not necessarily mean that you are intelligent in intrapersonal or interpersonal affairs. At the same time, it also means that one can learn and become more proficient in these areas. So, if you aspire for managerial or group leadership positions, it is necessary that you train yourself in different forms of intelligences that are related to these aspects of leadership.

TECHNICAL AND ORGANIZATIONAL INTELLIGENCES

Most human experiences require us to engage some or all of these intelligences simultaneously. In technical problems, it requires scientific intelligence. Most of us know, though, that problems require much more than purely technical skills. A director of a large corporate R&D lab mentioned that only 10% of projects in their Fortune 100 company failed due to flawed technology. Ninety percent failed owing to other reasons that included team dynamics, collaborative processes, understanding of what consumers really wanted, and marketing strategies, among others. Leading a successful team thus involves multiple kinds of leadership: What kinds of leadership roles an individual takes on depends on the evolution of his/her intelligences in these different areas. While an individual would perhaps be strong in certain kinds of intelligences naturally, others can be learned as we discussed in the previous chapter.

Figure 6.1 shows the kinds of leadership that may exist within your team, along with gaps in leadership. This is not an exhaustive list of different kinds of leadership needed in the industry. Others—such as leadership in vision or in personnel growth or market strategy—could be added to this schematic, depending on the exact nature of the program. Every program requires varying levels of competence in different aspects of

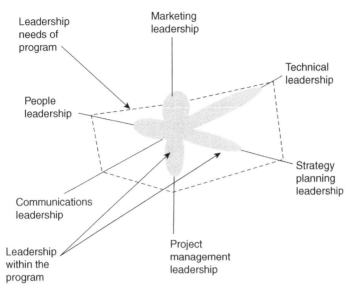

FIGURE 6.1. Example of different kinds of leadership needed by a program.

leadership. Depending on the goals and context of the program, it may have less needs in strategic planning leadership (for example, if the scenario is well understood and similar programs have been launched to address a larger need), in marketing leadership (for example, if that market is well understood), or in collaborative or people leadership (if majority of the group knows each other well and works well together). Alternatively, they may need high levels of leadership in these different areas.

Consider an example of a program to develop widget A. These include:

1. Leadership in understanding the situation and the needs as well as the strategy embodied in widget A that would make it successful.

2. Leadership in development and integration of technologies to make widget A.

3. Leadership in managing resources and project plans to meet timelines.

4. Leadership in understanding the motivation of various individuals in the team, their skills, and their abilities while ensuring effective communication and maintaining good collaborative processes.

5. Leadership in maintaining interest and commitment and managing motivation and expectations from stakeholders and supervisors of all members of team engaged in developing widget A.

6. Leadership in (a) development of manufacturing plans and (b) their implementation.

What are the key challenges in your team? What are major leadership needs that need to be fulfilled? Figure 6.1 provides a qualitative map of kinds of leadership needs and what is available within the team. Understanding this map for a given program or a team can help an individual strategically identify critical roles needed to be filled in the team. Even as a new employee, you can map key needs of the programs and where significant intelligence is needed to strategize and lead through critical challenges. As a new employee, it trains you to recognize the different kinds of intelligences and practice taking on challenges with your team related to these forms of leadership. For example, if there are key challenges with respect to market understanding and development of market strategy, it may be useful to participate in those discussions.

Even if your role is more narrowly defined to technology or product development, opportunities for learning these diverse forms of intelligence exist. Technical leadership requires you to help the organization's strategic goals through developing new science and technology, application of these new technologies, and guiding the team through decisions processes, as well as scenario analysis based on your expertise. All of these require strong technical intelligence. You will also have the opportunity to manage your project, interact with others (those who may be experts in adjacent domains and/or with those you collaborate), manage key stakeholders for the project and their expectations, and so on. These opportunities can help to improve your social and emotional intelligence.

In fact, irrespective of the program you are on, or your role in that program, you can have opportunities to lead and sharpen your technical, emotional, and social leadership skills. Let us look at a possible example of how this might work (See schematic in Figure 6.2). The core team from a business center may drive the development and commercialization of the program and includes product developers and manufacturing groups from the business unit. However, it must pull in experts from other parts of the company with expertise of new materials for

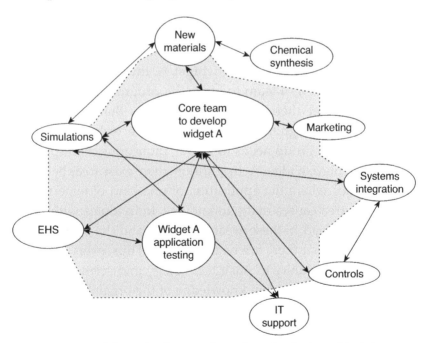

FIGURE 6.2. Schematic of a team focused on developing widget A.

widget A (who will work with the chemical synthesis group), systems integrators and controls experts, and simulations experts (all of which might reside in a central R&D facility). The core team needs marketing support along with support from the applications testing team (which is another group within the business center) and the EHS (environment, health, and safety group, which might be a corporate-wide group).

Members of a team located anywhere within this network shown in Figure 6.2 can have different opportunities to lead development of widget A. Widget A is a device that is new to the world that will help the company beat its competition. Thus, new materials systems must be developed or known materials must be applied in a new way to perform as per widget A's needs. Simulation techniques to achieve this require extension of existing expertise. Since it is a new system, controls and systems integrations are perhaps critical. Perhaps software for such systems already exists, and we need an IT company to apply it to this widget—so they are only consulting. While the core team is charged with developing and commercializing widget A, the whole team must work together as a team to make the program successful.

Given that there are numerous areas that require new inventions or significant extension of the technology, each individual or group needs to lead in pioneering its respective area to achieve widget A. In addition, there exist areas between disciplines where the application of one kind of expertise in another area causes many unknowns. Individuals within the team must lead in these areas to understand the implications and ensure that there are no unknowns. Thus, every member has the opportunity to push technology and science to areas outside the institutional knowledge of the organization—and maybe even the world—in helping to build widget A. There is also the need for leadership through teaching and advising. Each expert must teach other experts the implications of his or her developments so that design and implementations of this program proceed in synergy with the rest. Leadership also requires area experts to understand how their developments affect other aspects of widget A. This means that these experts go beyond their limited charter of "develop component x for widget A" and help design and develop a robust widget A. In addition, this collective of expertise must show leadership in making choices based on constantly updated learnings.

There may also be needs for exploration of areas defined by widget A that are common to all these efforts and that transcend the technical but are related. These include understanding intellectual property issues, understanding the market space and the value proposition based on cost, market, and technology considerations, environmental impact based on environment, health, and safety recommendations, and so on. These require skills in pattern recognition, competitive analysis, and research and development of strategic plans to win in this market. While these aspects of a project are often the responsibility of core team members and even outside consultants, these are sometimes less well defined and thus provide opportunities for leadership. These require rational or logical intelligence beyond just technical intelligence.

Clearly, with all of these interactions, this team of leaders must work with a robust collaborative process. Leadership is necessary to ensure that all the subprojects are progressing on schedule and on budget. When one or two critical components fall behind—and this often happens—the collaborative framework and the team of leaders must be able to account for it. A strong program leadership ensures that when certain components run into problems, other subprojects can be managed accordingly. It requires intelligence that is related to technical understanding of all subprojects, good administrative practices, attention to detail, and planning of logistics, among others.

We have already seen that an effort driven by a team of leaders also needs effective communication. If this is indeed a team of leaders and experts, an ultra-competitive atmosphere can quickly develop in the absence of effective communication and good collaboration practices. While it would be ideal for every individual to practice effective communication, it is rare that such a team can be put together. Invariably, a few individuals will have to ensure that effective communication is practiced by the team during this collaborative effort. Such leadership requires social intelligences—that is, recognizing people's needs, and how interactions can address these needs. It includes the ability to connect with people, resolve conflicts, and negotiate. This kind of leadership within the team also ensures appropriate dynamics within the team. In the absence of such leadership, widget A will probably not be successfully launched.

Thus, every project in which you participate provides opportunities for technical, business development, social and emotional development. You are exposed to a variety of challenges and you have the opportunity to practice intelligence skills related to these challenges and thus broaden your toolbox for effective leadership. Typically, individuals with a certain passion will focus on certain kinds of skills and allow others to address those that do not interest them. But as a new employee it is appropriate that you consider your own career goals and ensure development of all intelligences that are relevant to those goals in support of those leadership skills.

SOCIAL AND EMOTIONAL INTELLIGENCES

We are generally familiar with technical intelligences and how they relate to our job. Business intelligence has also been part of our recent discussions. We will spend some time describing social and emotional intelligence in this section and how they relate to our growth; often these intelligences are ignored even though they significantly affect industrial careers.

Various experts[41] have defined social intelligence as the "ability to understand the thoughts and behaviors of people (including oneself) in interpersonal situations and to act appropriately based on that understanding." Social intelligence[42] includes the ability to recognize and identify social situations as well as the ability to adapt to them dynamically and to draw on social component of one's personality—empathy, for example—for effective leadership. In today's relationship-based team structures, social intelligence drives the effectiveness of team performance. Social intelligent people are able to successfully perform cognitive and behavioral processes that include *social awareness, social acumen, response selection, and response enactment*. Socially intelligent people are able to

1. Be conscious of the details and nuances of a social relationship

2. Analyze accurately the implications of these nuances on the relationship and efforts driven by the relationship

3. Envision and plan the right set of behavior in the context of the social relationship aimed at meeting the goals of the group

4. Implement or act on the plans appropriately

---

[41]H. A. Marlowe, Jr., Social intelligence: Evidence for multidimentsionality and construct independence, *Journal of Educational Psychology*, 1986, **78**(1), 52–58; F. A. Moss and T. Hunt, Are you socially intelligent? *Scientific American*, 1927, **137**, 108-110.

[42]S. J. Zaccaro, Organizational leadership and social intelligence, in *Multiple Intelligences and Leadership*, R. E. Riggio, S. E. Murphy, and F. J. Pirozzolo (eds.), Lawrence Erlbaum Associates, New Jersey; J. Hogan and R. Hogan, Leadership and sociopolitical intelligence, in *Multiple Intelligences and Leadership*, R. E. Riggio, S. E. Murphy, and F. J. Pirozzolo (eds.), Lawrence Erlbaum Associates, New Jersey.

Daniel Goleman[43] is a lead researcher and expert in the areas of social and emotional intelligence. His methods to quantify these intelligences are considered to be among a set of benchmarks that corporations often employ to train their leaders. In a recent article, Goleman claims that researchers have found biological underpinnings for how social intelligence works.[44] Italian neuroscientists, he says, have found mirror neurons widely dispersed in the brain that fired only when the subject is empathetic to a stimulus—often to another being with whom the subject feels "connected." "This previously unknown class of brain cells operates as neural Wi-Fi, allowing us to navigate our social world. When we consciously or unconsciously detect someone else's emotions through their actions, our mirror neurons reproduce those emotions. Collectively, these neurons create an instant sense of shared experience."

This has significant implications to understanding of social organizing and leadership. It can explain how actions and emotions of leaders can arouse empathy and mirror actions from a larger group who feel connected with these leaders. This explains claims by numerous researchers that nonverbal cues often affect audiences more significantly than verbal content. How connected a community feels with the leader can become more significant than what the leader may say. Examples include audience reaction to how presidential candidates carry themselves being more important to voters than what they say. Researchers since the time of Kennedy elections have presented evidence that the audience often chooses its leader through empathy—how they connect with the individual style, presence, and posture.

[43]http://www.danielgoleman.info/

[44]D. Goleman, Social intelligence and the biology of leadership, *Harvard Business Review*, September 2008.

Researchers are said to have found neurons whose primary role is to detect other people's smiles and laughter and respond. Thus, a community will naturally respond more favorably to a leader who smiles more, and this will result in greater empathy with such a person.

Goleman's intelligence analysis attempts to study various components of a leader's social intelligence, including:

Empathy: Do you understand what motivates other people, even if they are from different backgrounds? Are you sensitive to needs of others?

Attunement: Do you listen attentively to others? Are you sensitive to moods and feelings of others?

Organizational Awareness: Do you understand social networks and are you cognizant of their unspoken norms? Are you sensitive to the cultures and values of the group?

Influence: Do you convince others by engaging with their self interests and involving them in discussions? Are you able to get the buy-in of key people in a decision-making process?

Developing Others: Do you provide feedback that helps people in the personal progress? Do you invest time, energy, and compassion into helping others develop?

Inspiration: Do you bring out the positive in others? Do you present a holistic vision that can draw enthusiasm and passion from others?

Teamwork: Is your mode of operation based on involvement of everyone in your team? Do you draw people into a cooperative effort by making them feel empowered?

Social intelligence becomes an increasingly critical component of leadership because social complexity increases with positions of increasing influence in the hierarchy. After all, at these levels, the role of a leader to define direction and lead based on trust and connectedness becomes increasingly more strategic and influential—and these can only be built through advanced social intelligence. At every level of leadership (and management), the ability to understand interactions between people (and one's own interactions), to understand the nuances of people dynamics, and to plan and respond appropriately is necessary. At higher levels of leadership, it also is necessary to understand the dynamics, interactions, and the culture of groups, because at these levels, one is often leading through relationships of and between numerous groups.

Goleman argues that being able to shape the social environment under stressful situations is perhaps the most critical factor in enhancing team performance. Through numerous case studies spanning corporate and noncorporate situations, he shows that leadership that shapes the environment to allow for greater human connectivity empowers the team to be more effective and successful.

An account manager in an IT company that provides solutions to health-care clients told us that the most important skill he sees in successful employees is based on their social intelligence. In this industry, technology differentiation between most employees is low. It is their ability to connect with their colleagues and their customers that helps them grow significantly. Their social intelligence helps them acquire, filter, and understand information from a large network of people, thus providing them with much greater input about changing markets, customer needs, techniques, and opportunities. In addition, they can also leverage this network to solve problems more effectively. For example, there are numerous cases where a colleague may be "on the bench" between projects. Being able to leverage their time can sometimes help solve a critical problem more quickly. In addition, this contact also provides for an opportunity where the favor will be returned.

Analysts[45] argue that such skills are important in technology-based large corporations. Often, extremely large companies are organized for efficiency. Often a group that is focused on product A will know little about product B or product C and the developments ongoing in those areas. Thus, numerous opportunities that could result from cross-pollination between these groups is lost. As the Merrill Lynch analyst Jessica Cohen once asked, "How is it possible that Time Warner owned both Warner Music and AOL and didn't create something like iTunes?" Such examples show that a culture of social connectedness is just as important as technical abilities. Social intelligence is key to building informal collaborations that allow for such cross-pollination, and companies that engender development of such skills and networks gain from them.

Another class of intelligence that is seen as necessary for good leadership is emotional intelligence. Mayer and Salovey[46]—two experts, among others, who have benchmarked emotional intelligence—define it as the "ability to perceive emotions, to access and generate emotions to assist thought, to understand emotions and emotional knowledge, and to regulate emotions reflectively to promote emotional end intellectual growth." Emotional intelligence is the ability of leaders to be aware of their own emotions as well as those of their group members, while using and managing these emotions to drive toward positive changes and to achieve (rather than inhibit) appropriate action. Emotionally intelligent people are "easier to work with." Understanding emotions can help an

[45]A. M. Kleinbaum and M. Tushman, Managing corporate social networks, *Harvard Business Review*, July 2008.

[46]J. D. Mayer and P. Salovey, The intelligence of emotional intelligence, *Intelligence*, 1993, **17**, 433–442.

individual understand how they might act because of the
emotions. It provides people the ability to make harder decisions knowing that they can understand people's emotions and
connect with them at a more emotional level to relate those
decisions. The same connection can also help emotionally
intelligent people inspire and lead more effectively.

Leaders who inspire and sustain inspiration usually have
high emotional intelligence. They are more able to facilitate
open-minded processes in planning or decision making since
they manage emotions in these processes more effectively.
Emotionally intelligent people understand complex feelings
and transition of emotions and hence have insight into what
makes people behave in different ways. They could be more
effective in managing communication to assess and address
emotional issues in people. Hence they are more effective
in leading people. Another trait in emotionally intelligent
people is the ability to handle stress, fear, or other emotions
and take appropriate action in a way that positively channels
that emotion. Thus, these people are not paralyzed by stress or
fear, nor do they get so excited that they make unfeasible
commitments.

Researchers point out that managers or leaders with emotional intelligence are more effective in the long term:

1. Employees are more willing to work for managers and
   give their best to managers with whom they favorably
   connect.

2. Senior people, as well as people with more experience,
   are often less willing to put up with managers who are
   not emotionally connected.

3. When managing groups, immature social and emotional
   intelligence can cause conflicts within the groups which
   affect performance.

Sometimes leaders can get away with being average or low in some facets of intelligence for some time as long as they are aware of those weaknesses and compensate through other strong facets of their intelligence. For example, they may have very poor emotional intelligence, but their technical intelligence, ability to strategically plan programs, and sociopolitical intelligence may help them actively compensate for their weaknesses—as long as they are aware of their weaknesses and find paths to deliberately compensate. However, even so, all facets of their intelligence will have to meet some threshold level.

A director in an IT company talked about a senior manager in his group. This manager was a key contributor: He had actively identified, developed, and maintained key customer accounts that accounted for over 60% of that group's sales. He was very successful in understanding the customer needs and driving his group to meet those needs. However, the manager himself was very frustrated that he had been passed over for promotion on numerous occasions.

He had rather poor skills in people management and strategy development. He over-promised to his customers significantly beyond people resources in his group and then drove his group to deliver. In addition, he did not prioritize his projects of plan strategically. He was constantly reacting to sudden changes in customer priorities. As a result, his group had high rates of burnout and turnover—more than double that in their industry. People in the group did not always have a clear idea about what was expected from them monthly. Often, he engaged contract employees for a specific task; and by the end of the month, the task had changed thus adding to the pressure and chaos. Eventually, some senior technical people in that group had their VP intercede and the manager was moved to a different group.

One cannot help recognize the despair in this case study. This manager had so much going for him, had he been willing to recognize his weakness in strategy development and in social and emotional intelligence. Companies value customers and dollars; this manager's ability to maintain those were a big asset. Had he been willing to learn a minimal level of emotional skills and ability to develop strategy, he could have reached great heights in his career.

Well-rounded leaders draw on all these intelligences to effectively drive an organization. This fusion of intelligences in leadership—sometimes termed successful intelligence— includes the usual notions of analytical intelligence, practical intelligence, and creativity. When confronted with a scenario where a program has not progressed as expected, a well-rounded leader can ascertain whether the hurdle is technical (some path may be unfeasible, perhaps), sociopolitical (one section of the team is unwilling to accept a certain path since it will undermine their own interests), emotional (one section of the team may have bad personal relationship with another), or a combination of these or some other. If inappropriately assessed, the solution proposed will not address the real (often unsaid) reason for the hurdle. Sometimes, the solution itself needs to be multidimensional. The strengths and weakness of leaders is defined by how well they identify, leverage, and apply their strengths while attempting to address and compensate for their own weaknesses. *Besides innate ability or talent in one or more of these intelligences, a strong leader can also draw on experience. Having been exposed to numerous similar situations provides this leader with a repertoire of possibilities she may be able to choose from.* Even if none of these apply, the breadth of experience in dealing with a variety of such problems requiring multiple intelligences provides templates and confidence for a leader to work through these.

In earlier sections we have spoken about simple, complex, and chaotic problems. That also applies to such problems requiring multiple intelligences, and this makes it more complex.

Sometimes these are problems that are simple with linear cause and effect. However, problems that include emotional and sociopolitical dimensions often do not have a single correct answer, and sometimes the answer may even be unknowable. Thus, experience provides the template to assess the scenario and respond appropriately.

LEADERSHIP AND NEW EMPLOYEES

The first few years with a company is the time and opportunity to gain skills and improve your multiple intelligences. Studies suggest that the success of a leader depends on the number of options he has in his repertoire to address any situation. If an individual knows of only one way to respond to a class of situations (say a colleague complaining about how he shares information), no matter what the nuances of each situation, the individual will only choose that way. As the individual learns of newer ways to respond to a class of situations (through either experience, coaching, or observing others), he will have more choices of how to react as well as learn to discriminate between these choices based on the nuances of the situation.

Even as a new employee, you will face situations that require you to recognize multiple intelligences in solving a problem. For example, when a colleague complains to you that she believes you are not sharing information appropriately, it requires you to understand the technical nuance of the situation (perhaps she would like more fundamental understanding or only a certain aspect that is critical to her work), the emotional nuance of the situation (perhaps she believes that you have shared important information with others that you have not shared with her), the political nuance of the situation (she might be from a different organization and there may be some proto- col with respect to information sharing), or the social nuance of the situation (perhaps you are friends and she expects that you share information with her before you share it with others). You might be required to respond to her in different ways based her perception and your past action. It might be appropriate to politely point to the predetermined protocol. Or you might have a relationship where you can sit her down, respond to her emotional needs, and then share the information you need to share. Or you might just hand her a technical report.

So how long does it take before you are a leader? It is not a question of time but what problems you are exposed to, what solutions you open yourself to, and what you learn. Any position of leadership often requires you to face numerous problems with different kinds of needs (technical, personal, emotional, business, etc.) that also require multiple intelligences. For example, these may include:

1. Conflicts between people in your group affecting progress
2. Low team morale
3. Technical challenges that require major new developments
4. Development of technology or business strategies
5. Management of projects to meet specific deadlines and deliver on goals
6. Resource crisis

Each of the examples listed above can have variations. For example, you might experience three different conflicts between people in your group, and all three may have different reasons and hence different sets of feasible solutions. How have you been exposed to these different problems and to variations of these problems? Were you involved in any of these problems? Have you had to find solutions in some cases? How did you react and how were they solved? Were they solved to the satisfaction of other stakeholders as well?

Thus, your development of leadership skills depends not only on what kinds of problems you have faced or have been exposed to, but also on ranges of solutions that are part of your toolbox—what you have seen has worked and what has not.

A manager in the R&D laboratory of a large "fast-moving consumer goods' manufacturer described to us the case of two employees who joined his group at about the same time. Both were highly trained scientists with PhDs who hit the ground running in terms of technology development. Vince had major inventions in the first year itself that led to a new line of products. Even the CEO at that time had samples of these products displayed in his office. Karen, on the other hand, laid the foundation of a new strategically important technology and essentially limited competitors' options to threaten a major product platform. While Vince's contribution was more visible (it brought significant amounts of profits to the company), he did not grow in the same way as Karen. Vince was promoted to the technical position he deserved; but despite wanting to take on management roles, he was not given an opportunity. Karen, however, was given numerous opportunities to take on more leadership responsibilities.

Leadership based on social and emotional intelligence was the primary reason for this difference. Vince was curt with people in junior positions, even if they did not report to him. He gave new employees very little space to grow independently. When his group members achieved technical successes, while he acknowledged their work, he gave them little opportunity to share their success with or get exposure to other groups or upper management. While Vince worked long hours, people in his group rarely did—unless Vince forced them to. People would find reasons to leave his projects.

On the other hand, while Karen did not come into the company with exemplar social and emotional skills, she respected people. She provided people in junior positions opportunities to define directions and run their subprojects, once the goals were defined, thus helping them build leadership skills. They often presented their work—and even Karen's work—at group meetings. They went out of their way to meet goals and often worked long hours voluntarily. A number of people grew to the next level within Karen's group, and they left the group to accept positions of higher responsibilities.

Upper management recognized that while Vince made more presentations to them, Karen was not only developing strong technology platforms but developing leaders who could also build technology platforms. They recognized Karen's ability to coach and to inspire people to do better.

After about 8 years in the company, Vince requested help from his mentor to understand why he was not being offered more leadership responsibilities. Through extensive coaching, he was able to recognize that his group members also had their own developmental needs that he was constraining through his working style and his personality. He began to work on those skills and over a period of two years, and he proved to his management that he could help people in his group grow and become leaders as well. Subsequently, he was recently offered his first management opportunity.

As a new employee, you have multitude of opportunities to develop these leadership skills from your projects. A qualitative indicator of these skills might be the tool shown in Figure 6.3. It shows that the space for multiple intelligences relevant to the industry is described by the vectors. An individual would describe his or her level of expertise in these different skills as shown by bold lines. Usually, for new employees, their strongest skills may be their technical acumen; for new graduates, though, it may not be as high as the figure

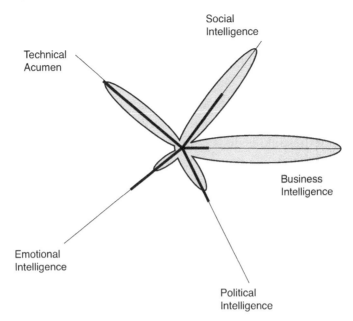

FIGURE 6.3. Development of your multiple intelligences relevant to the industry.

shows. The ellipses describe the intelligences most relevant to the marketplace. They may point you to your development plan.

How would you track your leadership development over time? To which of these dimensions have you been exposed, and in which ones have you had any experience? For example, were you or a colleague involved in a technical disagreement or a conflict? How was it resolved? How were you involved and what did you learn? Have you taken a lead in using one or more of these intelligences in solving problems? For example, did you need to learn new skills in one or more of these intelligences in solving a technical or a strategy problem? Answers to these might help you recognize your level of skill with respect to these intelligences.

Do you see yourself naturally skilled in one or more of these intelligences? Does feedback from your colleagues or your management team show consistency with your own assessment with respect to this analysis? This might provide one set of inputs to help you decide which skills you should specifically develop.

What are the skills needed for your next job in this framework of multiple intelligence (described by the gray ellipses)? Which of these skills does your organization most value? Does the organization or the market demand one skill more than others? Do you see that leaders with certain skills grow more efficiently? For example, in a high-growth area, perhaps the only thing that matters is technology and business strategy—all other skills are only marginally of interest. On the other hand, in a mature industry, with well-entrenched core technologies, perhaps the most important aspect is your network and relationship with customers. This should impact your development plans if you plan on growing within this industry. Are there gaps in certain skills across the organization, and do you see an opportunity to grow by filling that gap? These questions, along with your own career strategy map, should help you define your skills development plan.

Remember that the performance appraisal process that your company uses is the most accepted way to track your career and growth. Use the tool effectively to highlight your achievements. For example, if you have had significant learning in social intelligence owing to collaborative processes or conflict resolution that you lead, this may be a good place to document it. Similarly, if your project provided you with the opportunity to help develop business strategies, highlight your contribution. In addition, this tool may also be effective in describing your goals and getting buy-in from your management to support your development or provide you opportunities to practice leadership. For example, if you foresee that developing IP strategy will be a major need in the near future, you could include this in your goals and point out the learning and leadership opportunities involved. You could also list learning or development opportunities you would like—for example, an opportunity to understand your markets better and request your management support to help expose you to such opportunities. The performance appraisal tool thus becomes a powerful tool for your own development and training and can help to document and herald your growth.

THE FORCES AND YOUR CAREER

We started this book by saying that careers are defined by problem solving and that your growth within your career is affected by the nature and complexity of problems you choose to solve, how effectively you solve these problems, and the kind of skills you build to solve the next set of problems. In a technology company, various problems (or opportunities) present themselves. These could include:

1. Technical problems that lead to major inventions, new technology development, products, and so on. The bulk of problem solving is technical with some amount of social, political, and emotional problems solving necessary to effectively function and deliver the technical products. Most of the problems are linear or nonlinear.

2. Managerial problems to facilitate teams, organize resources, and prioritize and strategize development—problems that affect commercialization of a product or influence a small portion of the market. Or these could be problems around managing a technology. There is significant technical problem solving, but much of the problem solving is now social, political, and emotional. Some business skill development is also involved.

3. Business problems focused on understanding the markets and how internal resources and expertise can be

best leveraged to make profits. Much of this work is based on understanding of technology, but the major focus uses business intelligence and leverages social and political understanding.

4. Strategic problems that attempt to understand the market (or in more ambitious examples, certain portions of the economy), understand players in the economy, and change the dynamics of these players with respect to the market based on specific resources and technologies. Problems at this level are chaotic and complex.

While all of these problems are related to delivering profits, the nature of these problems is quite different and the jobs related to addressing these problems are also different. Managing your career is essentially based on (a) understanding the forces that come to bear on these problems and the jobs addressing these problems and (b) dynamically building skills and accessing new opportunities based on that understanding.

While your first job is technical, you can begin to learn the skills required to engage with the problems you find interesting to define your career. The book has attempted to help you build that understanding. As the windows of opportunity in a dynamically changing marketplace change, these skills allow you to continue to build your career. In Chapters 4 and 5, you explored exercises to broaden your technical skills to continue to explore and grow your career. The same dynamics hold true with business and organizational skills as well. The business nature of an industrial job always provides opportunities for those in the technical realm to explore skills in the realm of managing businesses. Such exploration can help improve your effectiveness as a technical leader in commercializing technology. On the other hand, it can also quickly lead to a career in business or organizational management.

Even as you begin in a technical role as a new employee, your job is in the middle of a large economy whose forces affect your career. Recognizing this also helps you note that in understanding how your job aligns with the company strategy, you can also impact the economy. How you impact it depends on the skills you choose to build and the problems you choose to address. It also directly impacts your career.

Let us take one last look at your job environment and what is expected of you; the schematic in Figure 6.4 is an example of what you might experience. It shows that your job function is within a team and under influence of a manager. The team, the company, the competition, and the world at large all influence and define your function, your goals, and your ability to succeed. How do you understand the scenario, fulfill your responsibilities (as expected in this scenario), continue to build

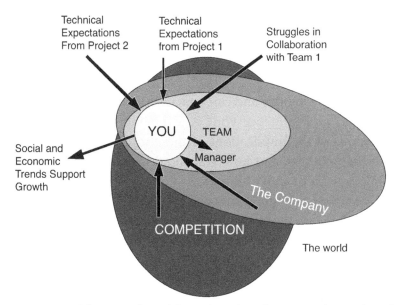

FIGURE 6.4. Schematic of your job at a given time, the context of your job, and stresses and pulls you experience.

your credibility, and subsequently grow? This is clearly an indeterminate system—there is no one right answer.

As you perform your job within this context, you have to address a number of forces. As per this example, we see the following:

- Expectations from you for projects 1 and 2.
- Struggles you may encounter in collaborating with teams for your projects. Perhaps there are conflicts in motivations, in how the goals are defined, or in the strategies being pursued, or maybe there are personality conflicts.
- Support from your manager continues to help your development.
- Continuing activities by competition threatens your ability to succeed in the marketplace.
- Changing social and economic trends in the world may be an advantage to you.
- Certain aspects of the company's policies or activities might stress you and negatively affect your success.

Do you recognize and can you articulate all the forces that surround and influence you? And having done so, are you conscious of the implications of these forces, their priorities, and their context, and how you should react to each of them while considering all of them?

Very narrowly, given that you are part of projects 1 and 2, do you understand the objectives of these projects? Are the articulated goals the most relevant goals within the context of the organization? Do you agree with those goals? Are your project goals and contributions aligned with the broader goals? From your perspective, are these the most important problems to which you can contribute? Are there bigger or more important growth opportunities for the organization that you ignore?

How do these problems relate to the strategy of the company in the context of the social and economic trends in the world? Are these problems and the strategy of your solutions based on your (or the team's) understanding of the strategy of the competition? How does it impact the competition?

Within the holistic context of your environment, if the two programs (that you are responsible for) are your biggest opportunities, it is most important that you are effective through those two programs. Do you understand how these two programs can solve key problems and help your company grow? Do you recognize how your work can impact the marketplace and address competitive strategies and your own company's growth strategy?

Within the context of the company's strategy, how have you and the team planned your project and your participation in it? Is it a high- or low-risk project? How do you know when you will be successful, and what is the probability of success? What are the timelines? Are there intermediate goals, and will they result in more sales? Will the implementation of this project result in or empower more products, resulting in more sales? Is this an isolated project or part of a larger set of projects? If so, what is your role in those?

How does your team understand and address all these questions? Have you and your team participated inclusively in asking these questions, and are all of you on the same page? If so, are you also in harmony on strategies planned and implementation processes? If not, what tools can you leverage to communicate your concerns effectively or influence the direction of the team appropriately? What has been your role in the team, and is that consistent with your goals and those of the team? Is a different role necessary for you (and in your opinion) for the team to be more effective? What can you do to play that role?

Have you accessed your network to truly understand these questions and get feedback? If, based on the feedback, you think you should be working on something else or if there should be a different strategy, how can you take advantage of your network to implement this or change direction? If your projects are not well-aligned with the company strategy and yet the project still needs to be implemented (and that happens sometimes owing to specific customer needs or market needs), what are the implications? Do you get lower priority or resources? Given this, can you leverage your network to be more effective?

A key member of your network is your boss. How are you communicating with her? Does she understand the context of your problems? Is she on the same page with respect to the context of these projects, their prioritization, alignment, and strategy, your roles in these projects, and the major concerns with these projects? What role will she or can she play in these projects? Can she influence the direction or effectiveness of these projects directly or through her network and are you engaging them?

What feedback do you get from your network, your team, and your manager? How are they different and where do they overlap? How does the feedback influence your understanding of the projects, the larger context, and your actions? How are you acting on this feedback?

How are you spending your time? What fraction of it is directly spent on the projects? What fraction is spent in ensuring that the teams are working effectively to address their goals? What fraction of it is in building and leveraging the necessary networks to influence your effectiveness? Given all your activities, how have you impacted all the various forces that act on your function: your two projects, the direction of the organization, your teams, your manager, your competition, and the marketplace?

In this exercise we have looked broadly at the context of all the problems and their interconnectedness, studied the key stakeholders involved and their role, focused on each of your projects, the strategies, the details of implementation, and their effectiveness, and then stepped back again to assess whether you are being most effective as a knowledge worker. In fact, over time, you should continue to go through iterations that focus in and then step back to take a broader look, thus ensuring that you are accounting for the details while at the same time you are not missing the forest for the trees. As you step back in again, you might find that the implementation must take a different direction. Or as you step back out, you might also want to ask yourself what the biggest opportunities are for you to take leadership roles. Are there areas of team dynamics that are weak? Is there something missing from competitive analysis to gauge what is truly happening in the marketplace? And as you ask these questions, continue to engage your network, your team, and your manager with your thoughts, respectfully asking for feedback. That helps keep them in the loop while making sure that you are making the best decisions at any given moment.

Your growth, your effectiveness, and your satisfaction with your job can only come out of what you are doing at the moment. You can strategize and plan—and they are important. However, all is for naught if what you are doing with your projects today is unimportant to you. Thus, use your projects today to learn, to grow, to show your leadership, and to be effective—in the context of your own needs and skills as well as in the broader context of the organization and the outside world.

SUMMARY

In any industry today, an individual's growth is based largely on her ability to help the organization grow. Often, that requires the individual to take bigger responsibilities in defining and scoping problems (whose solution can help growth) and then leading implementation of new solutions, probably in ways the organization is not set up to do. This is leadership, and it often requires multiple leadership skills to achieve this.

KEY TAKEAWAYS

1. Growth in a modern industrial environment often requires an employee to show evidence that she can take on responsibilities and challenges and scope and solve problems that are associated with a more advanced level of the hierarchical ladder.

2. The company, in hiring you, acknowledges that you are already a leader in your area of expertise. Even as a new employee, you start as a leader. Your first goal is to establish that aspect of leadership among your colleagues. Past chapters include extensive discussions on how you can achieve that goal.

3. Increasingly, industrial culture has begun to recognize and value teams of leaders, where every member of the team leads certain aspects of the team's venture. This allows the team to take advantage of the expertise and decision-making capability of every member of the team while allowing collective team wisdom to ensure that these decisions are in concert with overall team goals. This also allows for individuals to lead the team's efforts in specific directions. As a new employee, such an environment provides you with the opportunity to show your leadership skills—to truly understand a new area and its relevance to your team's goals, to scope a strategy with respect to this area and develop its implementation plan, and to get your team behind this plan.

4. An environment that supports a team of leaders allows you to lead with your technical expertise and then build your expertise in strategic planning, market analysis (or analysis of customer needs), project management, and implementation as you proceed, at the rate at which you are comfortable. It truly allows a new employee to practice leadership with guidance from senior colleagues while also providing him the opportunity to showcase his leadership talents.

5. Studies show that individuals are more willing to respect promises or commitments that they made voluntarily based on their own engagement with the problem. Individuals who have committed to such goals are often willing to stretch themselves to meet those commitments; and delays, when they occur, are owing to real hurdles and challenges and not mere excuses. This empowers a new employee to build support from colleagues based on rational analysis and data—support that a new employee could leverage to drive a new program or explore a new idea that may not have official support.

6. Effective leadership is driven by early understanding of a situation based on extensive research and recognition of patterns, identification of strategies based on scenario planning and analysis, the ability to engage with a team and facilitate a team consensus around both in a way that the team owns the problem, the strategies, the solutions, and its implementation. Promise-based leadership allows you to participate in all aspects of leadership.

7. An effective leader in the technology industry must have strong technical acumen; you are expected to recognize relevant technologies with respect to the

markets of interest, how competition and competitive technologies affect the marketplace and your company's role in the marketplace, and how you can manage these changes. You would then develop business strategy maps for your company based on its strengths and weaknesses while also understanding your competitions' strategy. These are roles that you can practice playing right away, within your group or project—recognizing and learning from the nuances in markets, development strategies, and so on.

8. Numerous business and cognitive experts now agree that industrial problems and their resolution—and hence leadership in complex situations—requires development of multiple intelligence (technical, business, social, and emotional, for example). These help you deal with different aspects of a problem and bring in solutions that recognize and are appropriate to these different nuances. Experts also agree that besides innate ability or talent in one or more of these intelligences, a strong leader can also draw on experience. Being exposed to numerous similar situations provides this leader with a repertoire of possibilities she may be able to choose from. Practicing leadership—by being part of or exposed to such challenges and consciously learning from them—helps build this repertoire.

9. As a new employee, your job is to practice leadership more than it is to lead. Practice leadership in different scenarios—where a project needs change of direction or where it needs to change speed, where it may require incremental changes in its processes or in its objectives, or where it may need to build revolutionary changes. What different decisions need to be taken, what social, emotional, and technical challenges need to be resolved,

and how good are you at implementing these? What do you learn from these different kinds of projects that help you broaden your leadership toolbox?

10. Use your performance appraisal tool effectively to highlight your achievements. In addition, this tool may also effective in describing your goals and getting buy-in from your management to support your development. The performance appraisal tool thus becomes a powerful tool for your own development and training and can help to document and herald your growth.

INDEX

Planning a Scientific Career in Industry: Strategies for Graduates and Academics
By Sanat Mohanty and Ranjana Ghosh
Copyright © 2010 John Wiley & Sons, Inc.